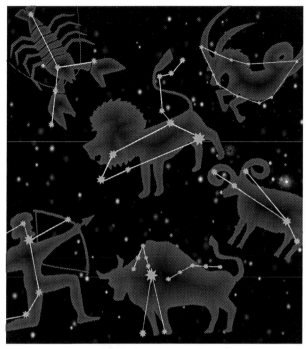

ZODIAC

PLYMOUTH

Edited by Lynsey Hawkins

GW00707742

First published in Great Britain in 2002 by
YOUNG WRITERS
Remus House,
Coltsfoot Drive,
Peterborough, PE2 9JX
Telephone (01733) 890066

HB ISBN 0 75433 550 X
SB ISBN 0 75433 551 8

FOREWORD

Young Writers was established in 1991 with the aim of promoting creative writing in children, to make reading and writing poetry fun.

Once again, this year proved to be a tremendous success with over 41,000 entries received nationwide.

The Zodiac competition has shown us the high standard of work and effort that children are capable of today. The competition has given us a vivid insight into the thoughts and experiences of today's younger generation. It is a reflection of the enthusiasm and creativity that teachers have injected into their pupils, and it shines clearly within this anthology.

The task of selecting poems was a difficult one, but nevertheless, an enjoyable experience. We hope you are as pleased with the final selection in *Zodiac Plymouth* as we are.

CONTENTS

Sheree McIntosh   1

Eggbuckland Community College
    Terry Robson   2
    Russell Smith   3
    Kirsten Godfrey   4
    Robbie Cumming   5
    Josh Crewe   5
    James Gill   6

John Kitto Community College
    Darren Moses   6
    Shannon Reynolds   7
    Liam Williamson   7
    Clement Murphy   8
    Lianne Cort   8
    Jodie Moore   9
    Kelly-Marie Brown   10
    Natalie Collins   10
    Gemma Eastel & Perry Whiting   11
    Carl Ranscombe   12
    Ross Davis   12
    Chris Chapman   13
    Kelly Hall   13
    Robert Bothma   14
    Vicky Dawes   14
    Gail Randall   15
    Kerryleigh Tills   15
    Daniel Hoare   16
    Lisa Crittenden   16
    Matthew Rawle   17
    Sammie-Jo Baker   17
    Daniel Eccles   18
    Lydia Roberts   18
    Leanne Arnold   19

Helen Richey	19
Dominic Perry	20
Gary Mills	20

Longcause School

Louise Cassidy	21
Jennifer Bush	21
Natara Clarke	22
Laila Innes	22
Rachael Tucker	23
Sam Stevens	23
Joanna Trigg	24
Alex MacQueen	24
Kylie Snowdon	25

Plymouth High School For Girls

Franciska Earle	25
Alison Wallace	26
Hannah Jarvis	27
Julia Hill	28
Daisy Langmaid	29
Emma Hemsley	30
Sam Ward	30
Gemma Bastin	31
Katie James	32
Katie Finch	32
Jennifer Bennetts	33
Kayleigh Herbertson	34
Vicky Palmer	34
Michelle Carne	35
Jenny Harris	36
Victoria Murphy	37
Stephanie Ayres	38
Jessie Coffey	38
Karla Anker	39
Lauren Chaloner	40
Kathy Chamberlain	41
Abigail Hurdle	42

Jenna Wald	42
Charlotte Cree	43
Sarah Manley	44
Shannon McCullough	44
Sophia Matthews	45
Emma Curtis	46
Abby Bennett	46
Hannah Moore	47
Amy Read	47
Emma Wager	48
Amy Gill	48
Jessica Weston	49
Belinda Seabourne	50
Sarah Adams	51
Naomi Lear	52
Rachael Elsworth	52
Laura Martin	53
Jessica Taylor	54
Hannah Godfrey	54
Keri Jolly	55
Siobhan Hodge	56

Ridgeway School

Victoria Wright	56
Laura Foster	57
Paul Hunt	58
Sarah Becs	58
Abi Pyatt	59
Michael Stanton	60
Billy Heale	60
Darren Franklin	61
Jessica Pike	62
Nikki Bredin	62
Melanie Standlick	63
Jamie Armstrong	64
Sarah Love	64
Michael Hagan	65
Carly McIntosh	65

Elizabeth Shaw	66
Amy Barrowdale	66
Ashley Morrison	67
William Amery	68
Jade Follett	69
Amy Lane	70
Bethany Bailey	70
Adam Steele	71
Matthew Moore	72
Matthew Rogers	72
Lee Chittenden	73
Natalie Jackson	73
Helen Maloney	74
Thomas Smith	75
Sarah Gaydon	76
Jessica Baskott	77
Anthony Boulton	78
Shaun Vinecombe	78
Nicholas Hunt	79
Helen Jory	80
Lawrence Turlej	80
Hannah Dolan	81
Deborah D'Arcy	82
Kyle Clarke	82
Liam Brett	83
Joe Higson	83
Shaun Jackson	84
Fawn Bennetts	85
Richard Vinecombe	86
Rebecca Mina	86
Danny Harris	87
Michelle Kendall	88
Natasha Garrad	89
Annette Goddard	90
Stuart MacManus	90
Kelly Temlett	91
Vicky Bawler	92
Katie Smith	92

Ashley McKenna	93
Jennifer Kelly	94
Jonathan Dodds	94
Matthew Elson	95
Daniel Wadman	96
Ben Challen	96
Kirsty Agnew	97
Kimberly Lewis	97
Rebecca Knight	98
Kirsty Barnett	98
Matthew Thornton	99
Laura Proctor	99
Kelly Vinecombe	100
Emma Pike	100
Kayleigh Ramsden	101
Becky Rixon	102
Fraser Tarrant	102
Sarah Rayne	103
Andrea Smith	104
Jayden Burton	104
Sarah Paull	105
Ryan Beasley	106
Daniel Gillings	106
Tom Barnes	107
Richard Weeks	108
Danielle Watch	108
Danielle McMullin	109
Kira Cartwright	110
Kylie Stonehouse	110
Sarah Barrow	111
Carla Fice	111
Justin Rule	112
Katie Bennatto	112
Jessica Fissler	113
Natasha Lane	113
Nicola Gaydon	114
Claire Geach	114
Cherish Kendall	115

Stacey Grix	116
Ashley Bennett	116
Adam Brooks	117
Gemma Fabiano	117
Emma Pearce	118
Thomas Brunskill	118
Jessica Loveridge	119
Charlotte Mifsud	119
Rebecca Morgan	120
Kayley Mann	120
Shaney Large	121
Claire Mullard	121
Natalie Harvard	122
Naomi Tucker	123
Daniel Grayson	123
Ben Johnstone	124
Lauren Palmer	124
Mikhaila Found	125
Martin Etheridge	126
Ruth Bennetts	126
Jordan Page	127
Laura Walker	128
Sasha March	129
Lucy Westgarth	130
Paul Sowden	130
Darren Edge	131
Aaron Perrin	132
Sarah Pengilly	132
Emma Rowe	133
Natalie Peters	134
David Foster	135
April Stephens	135
Lloyd Brewer	136
Christian Woods	137
Joshua Trust	138
Matthew J Draper	139
Luke West	139
Sarah Humphries	140

Martyn Welsh	140
Jack Gamble	141
Mark Cooney	142
Nick Bunczuk	142
Samantha Marlow	143
Kate Moss	144
Kayleigh Mackey	145
Emily Chapman	146
Nikki Houston	147
Emma Hagan	148
Rachael Gregory	149
Justine Bainbridge	150
Christopher Symons & Thomas Body	150
Rebecca Tomlinson	151

Woodlands School

Thomas Snell	151
Darryl Saunders	152
Victoria Cusack	152

The Poems

MY SISTER

Sporty and bubbly, laughing
All day long, she's small, but
Strong as a lion and fast as
A cheetah.

She enters a race to do the
100m sprint, she steps up to
The line slowly as if she's in
The Olympics.

She turns her head from side
To side looking up at the people
Above her. The gun fires and
They're off, people are shouting
And screaming 'Come on Simone!'

She wins the race and yet she's
Tired and over the moon.
The PE teachers Mr Piper and Miss Prifty
Come over and congratulate her.

Her face had turned as red as
Fresh tomato, then a cheesy smile
Appeared. The races have ended
And the track is closed, floodlights
Have been turned off until another
Event begins.

Sheree McIntosh (13)

MY MUM - THE GREATEST MUM OF THEM ALL

I remember my journey to the hospital,
It was the fracture clinic where I stopped.
Noises from a room nearby,
Was I shocked?
No! I've been here before.
Seeing my mum in her blue uniform,
Opening the door,
'Mr Wadling would you like to come in?'
That's when you see what's within . . .

The patients, the beds,
The tools, the doctor.
Tears are falling, children laughing,
'It tickles,' they say.
The doctor tells them, 'You're healed,
Go on your way.'
People chat outside in the waiting room,
They recognise their nurse from before.

It's my mum,
Do they know what she's really like?
Is she weird? Can she ride a bike?
No!
She heals broken bones,
With recycled plastic,
Plenty of colours, some pretty drastic.
Bright yellow, bright green,
This is my mum's dream.

A caring lady all her life,
A friend, a mother and a wife,
Eager to help, always there,
Giving tender loving care.

Terry Robson (13)
Eggbuckland Community College

SIR STEVE

Sir Steve, how well you row,
People see your power in the coxless fours,
Your brilliance never stops, you exceed many,
In the way you row your boat,
Never have you failed in all your glory,
You take yourself to the limits.
Can you teach me all you know?

Sir Steve, how hard you try,
You keep going, for winners never quit,
How hard it must be for a rower,
A rower with diabetes.
You carry on for five golds and beyond,
Soon you could row to the moon.
Do you realise the power that you have?

Sir Steve, how easy you make it look,
Do you stop? I think not.
You are the king of all rowers.
I really do envy your strength.
Your speed is divine,
I'd try and try, but I just won't catch you.
Can you row the Atlantic?

Oh, and Sir Steve, I remain,
With just one more question.

Can I have your autograph?

Russell Smith (13)
Eggbuckland Community College

A STEREOTYPE TEACHER

A teacher has a nerve system
A teacher has a brain,
A teacher is a strict person
Who carries round a cane.

A teacher gives you homework,
So you can't do anything fun,
A teacher is a mean person
And there's more than only one.

A teacher has a tidy desk
Which is always very neat,
A teacher will tell you off,
When you're rocking on your seat.

Teachers can be strict
Teachers can be kind,
Teachers can be mean,
Teachers could be fine.

Teachers are always different,
They could tell you off when you forget your kit,
But the worst thing teachers do is,
Give you a detention slip!

Kirstien Godfrey (11)
Eggbuckland Community College

I'D LIKE TO BE A LIFEJACKET . . .

I'd like to be a lifejacket,
And get carried all day,
Save people's lives,
And travel a long way.

I'd love to be lifejacket,
And live in a kitbag,
I'd never wash myself,
And never get nagged.

I'd like to be lifejacket,
When I inflate I wouldn't have to work,
Stopping people drowning,
People definitely wouldn't call me a jerk.

I loved being a lifejacket,
Being called a hero,
Lounging on beautiful yachts,
Until I got plunged into minus zero!

Robbie Cumming (11)
Eggbuckland Community College

GRANDFATHER

A rocky outline with human contours,
Swirling fog clouds, the vision of a gentle storyteller.
A rough hand on his carved wooden walking stick.
His white wind swept hair blowing back
To reveal his bright blue eyes that look upon his grandchildren.
Eagerly waiting for the end of his story,
They sit attentively in front of Tom.

Josh Crewe (13)
Eggbuckland Community College

TOGETHER WE STAND, UNITED WE FALL

We worked together,
We lived together,
We laughed together,

We were on the plane together,
We died together,
We lay together,
We'll be remembered together.

James Gill (13)
Eggbuckland Community College

ANANSI THE SPIDER

A nansi is a crafty spider
N ot your average one
A spider that can outsmart a tiger
N ot your web making spider
S mart he is with eight legs
I sn't he a friendly spider, you would think?

T he forest of stories he lives
H e is the smartest one of them all
E xcellent at outsmarting people he is

S lick and small that's him
P oking his nose in private things
I s so he can benefit out of it
D anger is here when Anansi is near
E very time you meet him he is kind
R eally he is the extra crafty one!

Darren Moses (12)
John Kitto Community College

FARTS

Some are so quiet
Whilst some are quite loud.
Some, they are hidden
While some are quite proud.
Some are done shyly
And some are quite bold,
You never know when one might unfold.
They ripple, they roar,
They bounce off the floor.
There are all sorts of farts
Loud, quiet, proud
And they make a weird sort of sound.
Sit down and think, of farts for a while
It might make you laugh, giggle or smile.
Dad's are the worst, you don't want to know,
If you do one yourself just go with the flow!
In some houses farts are forbidden
Unless you keep them very well hidden.

Shannon Reynolds (12)
John Kitto Community College

AN UNORGANIC SHARK

It has titanium teeth
Razor-sharp fins
Hearing like a radar
Skin like leathery thorns
Jaws like a diamond vice
It's the unorganic shark.

Liam Williamson (12)
John Kitto Community College

THROTANGULA

Awoken does the Throtangula,
A mist his screechy coven.
Blood gribbling from his clamping jaws,
And scratching with his dagger claws.
The roaring echoes throughout,
As his prey blafoons.
A thumping of his grapply feet,
And slobbering of his teeth.
Out the gristly hole he slimes,
To the fiendish sun.
He enters a grumbly village,
To penetrate his foe.
Enter town hall he does,
And snatches unkindly souls.
Grapples them with his grubbly claws
And sets off to the hollow hole.
Rip, thread, tear, dead.
He slaughters all his prey.

Clement Murphy (12)
John Kitto Community College

THE WRITER OF THIS POEM

The writer of this poem
Is as small as a stone
As healthy as a rabbit
And harder than a bone.

As faster as water
As clever as Tara
As silly as a sausage
As hot as the Sahara.

As loud as a radio
As loopy as a rat
As crazy as a scientist
As sneaky as a cat.

The writer of this poem
Has got a great big grin
She tries so very hard
To keep those giggles in.

Lianne Cort (12)
John Kitto Community College

A BEASTLY QUESTIONNAIRE

Do dogs dive?
Do rats rap?
Do birds barge?
Do cats climb?
Do puppies pounce?
Do guinea pigs grunt?
Do hippos hop?
Do fish flop?
Do dolphins dance?
Do people prance?
Do lambs laugh?
Are dragons daft?
Do robins rob?
Do jellyfish jog?

Jodie Moore (12)
John Kitto Community College

ART IS GREAT

Many different colours to create,
Pastels, paintbrushes and clay.

Surrealism and still-life are
Just two of my favourites.
Spiders and babies all in one place.

A swish and swosh here
And push and pull there,
Paint in your hair, clay in your nails
And colour dye all down your front.

But yes, you've guessed it,
Once you've left it,
You are left with a great masterpiece.

Kelly-Marie Brown (14)
John Kitto Community College

JUMBLED POEM

Its mouth as big as an apple
Its neck as long as a tree
With a pattern just like confetti
And eyelashes fluttering at me

It has a pouch as big as a handbag
Furry, just like silk
So many colours in the sun
It looks like a mosaic

It's fluffy and soft like a pillow
It's as round as a football
And it bounces like a space hopper
And it's as white as a piece of paper.

Natalie Collins (12)
John Kitto Community College

ANIMALS THROUGH THE DAY!

A nimals is what this is about
N ight owls come to scream and shout
I n the dark at about 10 o'clock
M onkeys swing from the treetops
A t about 6 in the morning
L ambs moaning and groaning
S weet little animals stuck in their homes.

T houghts of animals you may say
H ares and rabbits through the day
R ough rats go and bite
O nto and into the dark scary night
U can go to the zoo
G o into the field to hear the cows go moo
H ear the loud and quiet animals

T here's a lot of different animals
H eron is a water bird
E 'as a big neck and long legs.

D eadly as a dinosaur
A ll the lions stand and roar
Y oung and lively animals.

Gemma Eastel & Perry Whiting (12)
John Kitto Community College

FISHTIGEROO

Furry and stripy,
Bushy and curly,

Smooth as a pebble,
Yellow and shiny,

Bouncy and springy,
Bony and strong structured,

Bright as the sun,
Brown as chocolate,

Long neck like a giraffe,
Teeth like knives,

Flimsy fins like paper,
Hard shins like rock,

Bulging black eyes,
Whiskers like straws,

A catalogue for a fishtigeroo.

Carl Ranscombe (12)
John Kitto Community College

SPORT

S   port is an energetic thing
P   laying for the winner's cup
O   ther teams are better than yours
R   unning for the finish line
T   his cup should now be mine.

Ross Davis (12)
John Kitto Community College

THE QUIBBLESNIBBER

The Quibblesnibber is as bold as a wigolomb
He lives under the whiffling tree,
And eats the tum-tum fruits
He has small teeth and a big outgrabe.

He does not like the uffish birds
He eats them for his smidgin
He lives in Quilig with flogins
And eats people when the moon is mimsy.

Chris Chapman (13)
John Kitto Community College

THE RACE

Starting positions
Heart racing
Legs shaking
Bang! Bang! Go!
Running fast
Breathing heavy
Wind blowing
At last finished
Looking back
Who won?
It was
Me, me!

Kelly Hall (12)
John Kitto Community College

JUNGLE

Jungle, jungle, dark as can be,
It's all dark as far as you can see.

Strange, strange noises coming from the tree,
It gives us a scare so we all freeze.

Creepy, creepy spider,
Use your wits to outsmart tiger.

Tiger, tiger, orange as can be,
The jungle is your territory.

Leave, leave the jungle tonight,
Don't leave with a fright!

Robert Bothma (13)
John Kitto Community College

ROARING, BOUNCING GORILLA

A roaring, bouncing gorilla
A jumping, munching killer

Its sharp, scary teeth
Its long, hairy feet

Its long, fluffy ears
The lion never fears

This is a catalogue of a
Roaring, bouncing gorilla.

Vicky Dawes (13)
John Kitto Community College

IN THE JUNGLE

In the jungle
When he roars the ground rumbles
Searching through the trees
For a creature just like me
I am the king of the jungle
When I roar the ground rumbles
Watch me chasing
And racing
Creatures in the forest
I am hairy,
And I am scary,
Can you guess . . .
I am the best!

Gail Randall (12)
John Kitto Community College

ORGANIC POLAR BEAR

The polar bear's fur is soft and white,
Like pampas grass flowering heads,
Its claws are as sharp as rose thorns,
Yet his feet are as soft as ripe plums,
His eyes are as black and shiny as grapes,
Its nose is as wet as ocean waves gleaming in the sun,
Its ears are hidden by its fur,
Like squirrels' nuts in autumn.

Kerryleigh Tills (12)
John Kitto Community College

TIGER THE MAN

I'm big and evil that's what I am
I'll slice you into bits of ham
Everyone knows I'm the man
Because I'm a tiger with a master plan.
I'll slash and gash and rip and dash
I will kill you in a flash
Anansi is coming, oh no
I'll have to roar to see him go
I'm king of the jungle
I'm the jungle man
So here I am with . . . another . . . master . . . plan!

Daniel Hoare (12)
John Kitto Community College

I'M A . . .

I'm a dolphin, sleek and fast,
I'm a lion, fast, never last,
I'm a tortoise, always last - I hate that!
I'm a leopard, fancy that - I have spots!
I'm a tortoiseshell cat with spots and fur,
I'm a bear with fur and claws,
I'm a tiger with claws and I growl,
I'm a dog which barks and has floppy ears,
I'm an elephant with floppy ears and a trunk
I'm a . . .

Lisa Crittenden (12)
John Kitto Community College

HOW THE BEAVER GOT HIS TEETH

How the beaver received his teeth is a simple concept
Once the beaver had teeth the size of a toe nail
And was very good with his hands at woodwork
One day he was pottering around
When a man asked if he could help him re-do a kitchen suite
He accepted and he expected to be paid, but in the end he wasn't
Being a stubborn beaver, he asked for money, of course,
This wasn't wise due to the man being a *wizard*!!
Who had a bad temper and couldn't resist
In making his teeth as large as coconuts
This condemned him to cutting down trees with them forever
And his children and his children's children
And his children's children's children . .
That's how the beaver got his big teeth!

Matthew Rawle (13)
John Kitto Community College

DOLPHINS

D   olphins are the best
O   thers think differently
L   iving in the sea
P   laying in the waves
H   iding from the sharks
I   would love to see one
N   ice and friendly they can be
S   wimming in the sea

Sammie-Jo Baker (12)
John Kitto Community College

SHARK

The shark is the tropical predator of the ocean
They circle their prey to signal their death
Criss-crossing around the doomed prey
Never venture into shark-infested waters.

The faster they swim the more prey they catch
Their sharp teeth are deep embedded into their membranes
They cut through the water with their bladed fins
It truly is the predator of the sea.

Daniel Eccles (12)
John Kitto Community College

A BEASTLY QUESTIONNAIRE

Do dogs drool over dinner?
Do snakes slide on grass?
Do rats rap?
Do cats cry?
Do ticks tap?

Do penguins play with prams?
Are snails friendly with slugs?
Do dolphins sing with whales?
Do rabbits kiss racoons?
Do birds fly?
Can ducks cry?

Lydia Roberts (12)
John Kitto Community College

GOLD EAGLE MOUSE

Fiery red
A furry head
A big wing
As gold as a ring
As feathery as a chick
And is very, very quick
As round as a ball
And is very, very small
As scaly as a snake
Eyes as big as a lake
A catalogue
To make me a
Gold eagle mouse.

Leanne Arnold (12)
John Kitto Community College

A MOUSE IS A . . .

A mouse is a lightning bolt
A mouse can be dark as the night
Or white as the snow
A mouse is as fast as a bolt of lightning
Whoosh!

Helen Richey (12)
John Kitto Community College

THE POEM

What is a poem?
What does it mean?
Is it the meaning of life?
It's how you set the scene.

A poem is a key to life
A key to get away
From the worries of the world
And helps you seize the day.

You can be a hero
And save the day
Watch out for the bad things in life
Never . . . run . . . a . . . way.

Dominic Perry (12)
John Kitto Community College

EAGLE

Eagles are birds of prey,
They make their lives in mountains,
From ancient times people thought
Eagles were all power and courage.

Eagles sweep like aeroplanes,
Smooth as a piece of silk,
They build their nests of straw
And feed themselves with worms.

Gary Mills (12)
John Kitto Community College

HOLIDAY

I went to Sandy Bay,
For a week long stay.

We stayed in a caravan,
I wanted to work on my tan.

One day I went to the beach,
And I ate a lovely juicy peach.

I had lots of fun,
And enjoyed the sun.

I made sure I wore my sun hat,
And sat comfortably on a spongy mat.

I loved taking my dog Cassie on the sand,
Although she didn't like hearing the band.

Louise Cassidy (13)
Longcause School

FISHING

I was wishing I was fishing on a Sunday afternoon.
I had my fishing rod, bag and a pot of wriggly worms.

I've got my sandwiches and my coffee
Beside me on the bank.

I often come here fishing and sit upon the bank,
For if I was sat on the water I surely would have sank!

Jennifer Bush (12)
Longcause School

ANIMALS

There was an orange cat,
His name was Rusty Jack.

He liked to lay in the sun
And watch the world go by

There was a mouse
Who lived in next-door's house,
Who he had his eye upon.

But never could he catch that mouse
For he only had three legs!

Natara Clarke (13)
Longcause School

ART

My favourite lesson is art,
It is very close to my heart.

I like to use pencils and pens,
To share my things, with all my friends.

Painting pictures, makes me feel nice,
It reminds me of picking up sweet little mice.

Colour makes the work look good,
Art can sometimes be misunderstood.

Laila Innes (13)
Longcause School

ZOO ANIMALS

I went to the zoo on a hot summer's day,
I saw a ziggy zaggy zebra with a wiggly waggly tail.

In the next cage was the camel with the hump,
We moved towards the cheeky monkeys,
When one of them fell over a bump.

The penguins were swimming in the pool,
The giraffes stood under a tree to keep cool.

I went to see the big cats,
And saw them eating a rat.

The baboons were shouting and screaming,
When I decided I wanted an ice cream!

Rachael Tucker (13)
Longcause School

HOLIDAY

I want to go on holiday,
In the summertime,
I'll need to take my suitcase,
To carry in my hand.

I'm staying in a hotel,
It's five storeys high,
It's got a big, round swimming pool,
With a fountain on the side.

Sam Stevens (12)
Longcause School

HOLIDAY

I've got my swimsuit in my hand
Because I want to play in the sand.

I'll lay back and dream about
A nice big ice cream.

I'll play in the sand
With my bucket in my hand.

I'd like to play with my sisters
But now they're covered in blisters!

Joanna Trigg (12)
Longcause School

HOLIDAY

I'm looking forward to my holiday
I'm staying in a caravan at a Sandy Bay.

It was a sunny day and I went to the beach.
I was very hungry and I ate a peach.

We started to play a game of football,
When a boy called Alex tripped over a stall.

We walked over to watch a band.
I got tired because I had to stand.

Alex MacQueen (13)
Longcause School

JOKES

I like to read joke books,
I think they are fun,
Always offering other people a pun.

I like to make people laugh,
To fool around,
Making them think I'm a giraffe.

Jokes are a light relief, they take people's troubles away,
They tickle their fancy and hopefully make a smile stay.

Kylie Snowdon (12)
Longcause School

BULLIED

She sits alone in a dark room and weeps
The scars of her trauma shining through like blood.
She sits there in anguish . . .
Alone
    and
        desperate
As the salty tears brush her streaked face
She sits there like a frightened mouse
Not daring to squeak
For fear
If you were there,
Would you offer her your hand
In friendship
Or are you
    just
        another bully?

Franciska Earle (11)
Plymouth High School For Girls

This Night's Bedspread

White milk on a dark cloth,
The spread of clusters in an inky heaven,
A temperamental sun, a wise moon,
The star that rolls forward; midnight to noon.

Fickle satellites dirty, the velvet spread,
I watch as I lay softly to rest,
The dreams I will dream after a day in fields
The firmament listening, to my wishes it yields.

A deep plough twinkles in the pitched air
Pointing north, the centre of all travels.
I watch my twin brothers curled in their sleep;
The candles of Saturn they like to eat.

The duo of fishes that don't increase my flour or grain,
For bread that my family feed off;
The woman of water who crests the Earth
Pouring famine and disaster onto my turf.

The creatures that feed off the grazing she makes;
The goat, ram and bull of my land
The balance of rations fed upon two sage scales,
The starvation, the suffer when the arable fails.

And far away, to north of my farm
The sea a-lapping a soft shore
A crustacean or two crabwise the foam of the waves
And the scorpion watches alone.

The jungle close by, hides a golden lion,
I hear a noise, not of an ape, of chimp;
I tread softly and plait his mane as I near . . .
But it was the huntsman with bow and spear

And I, Virgo lady watch the creature's savage death,
From the portal window close to my bed.

Alison Wallace (13)
Plymouth High School For Girls

THE EVIL GRANDCHILD

My evil grandchild tormented me today,
On how I looked and that my hair was grey.
She hid my glasses and went wild,
Because she is an evil little child.

I'd tell her to go outside,
But she'd bully the other kids.
When she does colouring,
She leaves off the pen lids.

When she plays with her toys,
She rips off their heads.
Then goes to her room,
And bounces on her bed.

This girl of mine never ever is good,
Even though I wish, really wish she would.
Even though I have her for one night a week,
I have to make her soup; potato and leek.

I wish this girl could be gentle and mild,
But she isn't, she is my evil grandchild!

Hannah Jarvis (11)
Plymouth High School For Girls

REALM OF THE REAPER

A frozen sky
On an icy morn,
Reveals the earth,
Deathly forlorn.

A snow-tipped spear,
Bearing cruel frost,
Leers with destruction,
At the life which is lost.

Snow heaped high,
With carcasses of the dead,
Fear and winter
Newly wed.

Death lingers on,
As do misery and cold,
Fresh born babes,
Die like the old.

Menacing clouds
Billow over the sea,
The frost creeps out,
Like the boughs of a tree

At the end of the darkness,
A light appears,
A beacon of hope,
That casts off all fears.

The rays of the sun,
Awake and arise,
Delivering life
To the world,
Its prize.

Julia Hill (11)
Plymouth High School For Girls

JOURNEY OF YOUR IMAGINATION

A hazy heat shines above the water,
Lit by glittering sparkly waves.
A lonely seagull wheels up high
Skimming towards the caves.

There are mermaids in this azure blue
With tails of pearly cream.
They hide away till midnight,
And sing while I'm in dream.

And while in dream and slumber,
I sail up to the moon
In a yacht of broken seashells
And a sail of homespun tunes.

Travelling on the moonbeam
I float to many lands.
Of spicy bronzen deserts
With trickling rolling sands.

In India I travel on,
To a forest dank and dark
Where stretching tigers sigh and yawn,
With the mouth of a great white shark.

This is the land of Hindu gods.
Mottled with a sky blue tan.
Basking in their magic
And moving the world of man.

While they play their mischief,
I sail back to my home
And slip into the blankets,
Curled into fleecy foam.

Daisy Langmaid (13)
Plymouth High School For Girls

STAR RIDE

As the sky turns dark, the light creeps away
I begin my search to faraway
I jump upon the Taurus back
And begin my search for the zodiac
My many questions seek an answer
Shall I ask Leo, Libra or Cancer?
As I travel further across the sky
I meet the Gemini
The stars still sparkle a dazzling show
I pass Aries and Scorpio
We have started to travel away afar
We have no idea where we are
Virgo gives us some assistance
She guides us off into the distance
Pisces and Capricorn lead, as they must
Then we reach Aquarius
Sagittarius takes us to the end
Oh I wish I could take this journey again.

Emma Hemsley (11)
Plymouth High School For Girls

THE FOUR SEASONS

The trees are budding,
the weather is getting warmer,
Lambs are born and eggs are laid,
Easter is coming up.

The leaves are all out,
The weather is hot,
Birds are singing,
Children are playing.

The leaves are golden, brown,
The weather is getting colder,
Birds start to fly away to warmer climates,
Harvest has arrived.

The leaves are falling off,
The weather is cold and wet,
Animals are hibernating,
Christmas is nearly here.

Sam Ward (11)
Plymouth High School For Girls

ZODIAC

As I gaze up to the starry sky
I see a star go flying by,
I make a wish so I can see
Past the stars and sky with thee,
As we shot off to the stars
Right past Venus then past Mars,
We came across a star never seen
We had to go, we were so keen,
Then I saw a zodiac Sagittarius and Taurus too,
I wonder which one belongs to you?
Mine is Sagittarius but I wish it wasn't.

Then at the break of dawn
The wind rushed by and the world of stars was left behind,
In my bed I lay dreaming of the zodiac signs
I saw that night in the sky of stars,
Past Venus and even Mars.

Gemma Bastin (11)
Plymouth High School For Girls

THE FACE IN THE WINDOW

I entered the house,
I heard a sound, a bang.
Was it a mouse?
My heart missed a beat,
What was I to do?
What would I meet?
A shadow was near,
I couldn't move.
I was filled with fear.
I felt something cold pass over me,
What was it doing?
Who could it be?
I was shaking like mad,
I scrambled outside,
I wished I was safe at home with my dad,
'Help, help,' I cried.
I ran away from the place,
I looked behind.
And there was a face.
Was it just my mind?
A terrible thought came into my head,
That was my uncle, uncle Ted,
But wasn't he dead?

Katie James (12)
Plymouth High School For Girls

SKY FLYER

Like an eagle swooping down for prey,
Feathers like silk ruffled by the breeze.
Climbing high cliff faces, flowing like a long reel of ribbon.

Talons outstretched, sharp and deadly,
Its beak pointed like an arrowhead, glinting in the sun.
Magical and mysterious like the pool in an eagle's eye.
Its elegant spirit gliding through the skies, as its memory lives on.

Katie Finch (11)
Plymouth High School For Girls

AUTUMN IN AMERICA

The fall . . .
Misty mornings,
Golden leaves,
Children playing,
Back to school.

The fall . . .
Busy people,
Off to work,
Crowded airports,
No one aware.

The fall . . .
Twin towers,
Ruined remains,
Twisted metal,
Fires blazing.

The fall . . .
Anger growing,
Preparing for war,
Chaos reigns,
Dark times ahead.

Jennifer Bennetts (11)
Plymouth High School For Girls

WHO AM I?

I am a rebel
My principles mean all
If you will stand against me
I will make your country fall

I am the victim
I've lost my family,
My mother, my father, my daughter, my son,
There's no one left but me

We are the government
We'll take this in our pace
We will find out who did this
And kill them off without a trace.

But we are the people
And in these days of plight
We shall stand together
Our country shall unite.

Who am I?

Kayleigh Herbertson (13)
Plymouth High School For Girls

ZODIAC

As I look up to the starry sky
I see my dreams go sailing by.
No one knows what it's like to be me,
My zodiac is all I see.

I'm all alone in this universe,
It feels as though my life has been cursed.
My zodiac to me is pure magic,
But then to others it's all quite tragic.

Then as I draw nearer my dreams seem so bright,
At first it can be such a fright.
It is only then that I can see,
My dreams and my zodiac are both in me.

Vicky Palmer (12)
Plymouth High School For Girls

GOD'S DOVE

What is life?
Why are we here?
Nobody knows
Until he is near.

What is it like?
Straight up above
Into the wings
Of God's big dove.

Where is the place?
That most people go
Is it quite far?
I don't know.

We will not see
Until it's our turn
To leave this life
And never return.

When it ends
I hope I'm loved
And taken to the wings
Of God's big dove.

Michelle Carne (14)
Plymouth High School For Girls

THE GUMMYGOOT

The Gummygoot lurks round the u-bend,
Of the toilet tube with the grime,
He lies in wait for night to fall,
To slither up in slime.
He leaves a trail of silver dust,
And makes a squelching sound.
He likes to suck up hair and mud
That lies upon the ground.
He creeps down the plughole,
And slides down leaking pipes
He oozes down the sewage works
And gives the rats a fright.
He floats along with the rainwater,
With the coke cans and bits of crumbs.
Slurping up dead leaves and twigs,
And tacky bubblegum
When he reaches the pipes end,
He is in the sewage works.
Being squeezed through machines
With all the muck and dirt.
Soon he's back in the pipes,
Floating with the flow
Polluting now fresh water -
He is swaying to and fro.
He leaves his stream of silver dust
And trail of slimy goo,
As he returns to his home
The gooey-gungey loo.

Jenny Harris (12)
Plymouth High School For Girls

FISH

A musical fish swam in the sea,
With minnows and with whales,
Until his mum said, 'Time for tea,
And afterwards practise your scales!'

He swam through the coral,
He swam through the weeds,
He dodged all the others
At tremendous speeds.

The fish arrived home
Just two minutes late,
To find a cross mum
And an empty plate!

His brothers and sisters
Had eaten his meal,
His favourite dish
Of barbecued eel.

Then to his mum
He put his plea,
'The food has all gone,
What about me?'

'Don't worry my dear
Because you see,
There are still plenty more
Fish in the sea!'

Victoria Murphy (12)
Plymouth High School For Girls

THE CRY

Alone,
Ever wondering,
Always fearing.

Everywhere,
I hear,
The person screaming.

Always,
Everlasting,
Always dreaming.

Ever,
A darkness,
Forever leering.

Forever,
The screaming,
In the dream.

Stephanie Ayres (13)
Plymouth High School For Girls

ZODIAC

An imaginary strip stretching across the sky,
An image so far away into the distance,
A glisten, glimmer, a glitter and sparkle,
Spheres spiralling round and round.

A strip divided the twelve symbolic zodiac signs,
Each which has a special representation,
Each sparkling sign is printed into the sky
Full with a wave of shimmer.

Floating in their dainty shapes,
Each with his very own special name,
Making their important influence on people,
Looking down on us from their position above.

Everyone has their own astrological feeling,
A symbol of the picture you can see
That may be a hundred light years away,
Far away into the future, the distance.

Jessie Coffey (12)
Plymouth High School For Girls

A POND'S LIFE

The pond is alive, breathing new.
Fish swim around, getting on with their daily lives.
Nobody knows this pond,
It's a secret unknown water expedition.
Hidden, deep in the pond surrounding, are frogs and
                              and tadpoles having lunch.
The pond is found. Glimmering in the sunlight,
People surround the helpless pond and devour their picnics.
As they leave they dispose of their rubbish on the pond's
                              banks and water.
They don't care.
The pond gets filled in; for houses.
They, the government say protect the wildlife,
Instead, they are destroying it.
They command the existence of rivers, ponds and lakes.
Because of them, the lovely pond exists no more.

Karla Anker (11)
Plymouth High School For Girls

THE MARY CELESTE

The Mary Celeste sat in the gloom,
The water lay still, promising doom,
The air was eerie, quiet and crisp,
As came a grey and rolling mist.

Nobody stirred upon her deck,
The ship appeared as a silent wreck,
Silver moonlight showed the sight,
As shadows cast a ghostly light.

Everything was left right there,
Nobody had a rip or tear,
It looked like they'd all disappeared,
As if each one had, had great fear.

A deck of cards was left, unplayed,
Two unpacked chairs were softly laid,
Upon the wooden dark grained floor,
Lit from a candle behind a door.

Where those sailors ever went,
Was what the people who were sent,
Said as they did search and look,
Not having even a glimpse of luck.

And still the mystery goes on,
Because the people found were none,
As to what happened that night,
To make the sailors flee the sight.

Lauren Chaloner (11)
Plymouth High School For Girls

OUR STREET

There are many houses on our street,
If you take a walk down it,
You just could meet:

The Taylor twins,
So jolly and gay,
They are always having picnics,
On the coldest winter day.

Miss Gribblebooth,
The grumpy old dear,
You could catch her at the pub,
Drinking whisky or a beer.

Mr Pistachio,
That shy little nut,
You might see him in his garden,
In his funny little hut.

The Evans family,
How wonderfully rich they are,
They're often seen out and about,
Showing off their newest car.

Maggie and May,
What sweet little girls,
Their mother dresses them to match,
Right down to their pretty little curls!

Kathy Chamberlain (12)
Plymouth High School For Girls

THE DOG

He lies carelessly,
Head rested on his paws,
Watching the world go by,
At his rope he tugs and gnaws.

His big sad eyes stare up at the world,
His elegant tail wrapped around him,
His body becoming skeletal and thin.
His velvety fur, soft and smooth,
And his whispery whine so silvery and soft.

But one day as I walked along the grey road,
No puppy there for me to love,
Nothing,
He was gone.

Abigail Hurdle (11)
Plymouth High School For Girls

MONSTER MIST

Mist is like a dark grey curtain,
Hiding the world
From the human eye.
It casts a creepiness
Upon the world.
People go through the mist
And disappear.
I wonder
If animals like it
Being hidden by the silent, creeping,
Monster mist.

Jenna Wald (12)
Plymouth High School For Girls

FROM A CHILD'S POINT OF VIEW

I'm spinning and kicking,
I'm dancing with the trees,
I'm leaning on the fence, my bar to rest.
The green of the grass -
The soft of the mat.
The holes in the hedge,
Merely my cupboards.
The windows - my personal view
Into my private place,
Only for me!

Coming back now,
All I see is leafy trees
And green, green grass.
A cold hard fence,
The cupboard I once saw,
A series of rabbit warrens,
My private place, to hide
From the world, is gone, it's just
The window, showing me
The living room.
What've I lost!

I've lost the joy
Of obliviousness to the world,
The imagination that saw:
Holes in hedges as cupboards
And green grass as mats.
I've lost my hidden and private place
That hid me from the world.
But most of all,
I've lost my childlike innocence.

Charlotte Cree (13)
Plymouth High School For Girls

LOOKING OUT OF THE WINDOW

Looking out of the window
What do I see?
I see the sunlight shining
On an apple tree.

Looking out of the window
Now what do I see?
A cat watching sparrows
Feeding in the tree.

Looking out of the window
Oh no! Now what do I see?
The cat eating a sparrow
That was feeding in the tree.

Looking out of the window
Now what do I see?
The cat licking his lips
Underneath the tree.

Looking out of the window -
I suppose that what I see
Is all of the components of natural history.

Sarah Manley (11)
Plymouth High School For Girls

TORN

An old lady stood all hunched over,
Not moving a single muscle,
She was a scruffy torn old lady,
Yet, she stood with a smile,
Almost frozen, waiting . . .
In a world of her own.

An old lady still all hunched over,
Wasn't moving a muscle,
She was dirty and filthy,
Yet, had a smile full of sweetness
Almost waiting in a frozen style
In a world of her own.

Shannon McCullough (11)
Plymouth High School For Girls

MAISY

Blue eyes bright,
Feet snow white.
Siamese - if you please.
Prancing, dancing,
This way and that,
My little pussy cat.
Tormenting, unrelenting,
Billy my Yorkie sighs,
Always watching, always playing.
My little blue eyes.
Born so small,
Because quite ill.
My dad nearly fainted,
At the sight of the huge vet bill!
Goodness knows how,
She's all right now!
My little blue eyes.
Maisy, little kitty,
Always bright and pretty.
My sweet little Maisy.

Sophia Matthews (12)
Plymouth High School For Girls

CHOO-CHOO MAN

He blows out smoke,
And yells every now and then.
He makes a lot of noise,
But he is really quite shy.

His bright green coat shines in the sunshine,
And his gold fastenings glitter.
His round face smiles widely,
As he stops at his house.

He takes people on rides,
His legs running faster and faster.
He toots to make the ladies jump,
Then covers them in a thick blanket.

Some may say it's silly
To give him a name.
But he just smiles proudly,
My very own choo-choo man.

Emma Curtis (11)
Plymouth High School For Girls

MY POEM

P oems are created from your imagination and formed in your mind.
O riginal poems are always best, from the heart, from experience.
E ach poem is individual and about different things.
M ost poems are very different, some are made up and others
    are from journeys and the past.

Abby Bennett (11)
Plymouth High School For Girls

THOUGHTS OF WHITSANDS

Happy thoughts of Whitsands
of sand and sea and sun
of swimming in the clear blue sea
and having so much fun

With friends to play
we spent the day
with kites, canoes and laughter
we ate our sandwiches on the beach
with baked potatoes after

Summer now is over
with all its outdoor fun
our holidays have now ended
oh how I wish they'd just began.

Hannah Moore (11)
Plymouth High School For Girls

NEVERMORE

Hither and thither she paces the green,
Heartless and forlorn in lunatic fashion,
She calls,
Calling for the loved one nevermore shall she see,
Feared dead, killed in action was he.

Amy Read (11)
Plymouth High School For Girls

SILENT STARING

So there I was,
Just sitting there
Nothing to do,
But stare.
Stare into an empty space.

The room was silent,
The air was still.
There was no movement,
There was no sound.
The room was empty,
Silent, still.

Emma Wager (11)
Plymouth High School For Girls

GERMS

Germs,
They squirm
And wriggle inside you,
I wonder what those germs are up to?
Mum says I should take more care,
Because those germs are everywhere!
Maybe she's right,
Those germs can fight!
They can give me the flu,
They can give it to you!

Amy Gill (11)
Plymouth High School For Girls

ANIMALS, ANIMALS

Animals, animals, everywhere
in the sea and in the air.
Animals here, animals there
animals around us
everywhere!
Some are scary
some are sweet
some are down below our feet.
Some are quiet
some are loud
some live here and some live there.
But where?
A few have scales
a few are as big as whales
some live in water
some live in air
all of them different
not one the same!
But where are they?

Everywhere!

All live in different habitats
some thin and fat
some as small as rats
some with wings like bats
some horrible and slimy
some really tiny.
Animals, animals, everywhere
you look and where you stare!

Jessica Weston (11)
Plymouth High School For Girls

I WENT TO THE ZOO TODAY

I went to the zoo today, I saw lots of animals,
I went to the zoo today, I saw all of these.

A is for antelope, sniffing around for ants,
B is for baboon, showing how they dance,
C is for cats, not domestic of course,
D is for dogs, as big as a horse,
E is for elephants, all called Elly,
F is for foxes, with a pretty thin belly,
G is for gorillas, like to do nothing but sit,
H is for hare, almost a rabbit,
I is for iguana, changing colour all the time,
J is for jaguar, I wouldn't want one to be mine,
K is for kangaroos, jumping around,
L is for limas, they make a funny sound,
M is for monkeys, the cutest thing you've ever seen,
N is for narwhale, a whale pretty mean,
O is for orang-u-tang, swinging from tree to tree,
P is for penguins, who live near the cold sea,
Q is for quail, hides in its shell,
R is for rabbits, foxes are its idea of hell,
S is for snakes, makes quite a cool pet,
T is for turkey, as slow as it gets,
U is for under the sea, a whole new world begins,
V is for vulture, with its huge wings,
W is for wildebeest, truly wild,
X there is X, so I lied,
Y is for the younger ones, who can't bite,
Z is for zebra, striped black and white.

Belinda Seabourne (13)
Plymouth High School For Girls

IN MY MIND

In my mind I see a garden, fresh with the smell of spring.
There the leaves are as green as the sun is yellow and the sky
                                    as clear as water.
At the bottom of the garden is a pond, with wildlife
                              beyond imagination.
There are frogs and frog spawn, lizards and salamanders,
Even a few mammals, like deers and mice come to the water's edge,
All animals drinking, slurping, eating, jumping and frogs suddenly
dropping with a splash and a plop down to the bottom to take a chunk
out of the dark green, sticky algae that lies at the bottom of the pond,
at the bottom of the garden.
By the back door lies that dog stretched out and the cat curled
                                    up next to it.
Guinea pigs and rabbits roam free filling their tiny stomachs with
large amounts of long luscious green grass that covers the garden.
Peace is what I see.
Just then a swarm of bees would come buzzing by,
Looking like formations of shapes and letters.
Next a flock of birds coming squawking by,
Flapping their large wings like sails on a boat, on a windy day.

Then as I enter the garden, as the gate creaks open,
It stops. It all stops.
The croaking, slurping, splashing, plopping, buzzing,
Flapping, squawking all stops.
The beautiful garden I once saw, was no more,
Just a garden with a pond and a back door.

Sarah Adams (13)
Plymouth High School For Girls

COLOURS OF AUTUMN

Glowing, golden leaves.
Creamy clouds.
Bare, brown trees.
Dramatic dahlias.

Frost, silver, shiny.
Burgundy bonfires.
Blue blackberries.
Rusty russets.

Milky moonlight.
Pale, shafting sunlight.
Magical midnight.
Colours of autumn.

Naomi Lear (13)
Plymouth High School For Girls

I AM THE WATERFALL

I am the waterfall
I trickle over the rocky caves and fish.
I use myself as the beauty of the forest
I think I am something like an ornament
To show people what rights we have in the forests
What do I do? Where do I go?
I do not know what to do, for I am the waterfall.

Rachael Elsworth (11)
Plymouth High School For Girls

THE FIELDS OF HOME

At seven in the morning, up I'd get,
Fully prepared for a hard day's work.
I set out to collect my 'work mates',
And we would head off,
Talking about our business plans.
We were happy.

At eight in the morning, we arrived at work,
Just two minutes after leaving home.
We walk across the green carpet to the office,
And start off, hard at work.
Cutting down branches, hacking at leaves,
Flattening grass, then resting in the breeze.

It's midday now, and time for lunch break,
But we are back again at one.
Stamping, breaking and cutting.
Making 'chairs' and 'tables' and 'shelves' for storage.
Then we stand back, and look at the finished masterpiece.
Our den! Everyone smiles.

Then we do a workout, running through the long grass,
Trying to catch each other, 'chasies'.
But soon we are tired, so we rest in the den,
Eating biscuits.

It is six o'clock, dinner time, work is over for the day.
We say goodbye, then we depart.
Five year olds, we are still young.
Early to bed and early to rise.
Ready for another day.

Laura Martin (13)
Plymouth High School For Girls

ZODIAC

Thin and fat,
Small and big,
An ox, a rat,
A horse, a pig.

More animals came,
To join in the race,
For the year would be named after them,
If they came in first place.

Into the river,
A splash and a splish,
For all of the animals,
To win was their wish.

The rat was the quickest,
And soon he had won,
The other animals finished slowly,
As they came in one by one.

Jessica Taylor (11)
Plymouth High School For Girls

THE MIRROR

The reflection that you see,
Is not as it appears to be,
As beautiful as it may look,
They're not as open as a book.

The mirror could be wrong,
The person may look long,
Just look inside,
They may just hide.

The image produced,
Is not to be improved,
The person looking in,
Might just have no wonders within.

But as they show more,
The person they adore,
Slowly dies away in vain,
Never to be seen again.

Hannah Godfrey (12)
Plymouth High School For Girls

LOVE

The feeling which binds a broken soul,
The passion that finds a lost heart,
An emotion yet to be discovered,
A burning and beautiful part of life.

Yet it is deep and desolate,
It calls to you in your sleep,
A scratching in your empty heart,
It's painful and people fear its power.

How can something so soft and gentle
Demolish your feelings for others,
If it is so kind and caring,
How can it rip your heart to shreds?

Keri Jolly (13)
Plymouth High School For Girls

DREAMS

Dreams can be heavenly
Dreams can be nightmares
But the best dreams of all
Are the ones that you call wishes.
A dream can be a wish
A wish can be a dream
As long as your heart knows how to do it.

Siobhan Hodge (11)
Plymouth High School For Girls

KUBLAI KHAN

Lush, green grass,
Windows made of coloured glass,
Streams that flow,
Over mountains high and low.

Inside carpets made of silk,
With little kittens drinking milk,
Pillars standing proudly,
With bands playing loudly.

Golden apples upon the trees,
Buzzing around them yellow bees.
As I watched kites soaring,
I know this dream wasn't boring,
As I saw them flying high,
There was a lovely smell of apple pie.

I heard many people cheering,
This gave me a lovely feeling.

Victoria Wright (13)
Ridgeway School

ALCOHOLIC

Love touched us one time
You said we'd last a lifetime,
Instead you let the drink
Dominate your life.

You pushed me away,
I didn't understand,
So I couldn't help.

I found you that morning,
The smell of vodka on your breath,
Slumped over the table, whining
Yet, words wouldn't enter my mouth.

I searched the room that day,
Do you know what I found?
Drink was obviously what you now lived for,
I needed to see for myself what you had turned into.

You started emptying out the drawers
Looking frantically,
Hot, sweaty and frustrated,
With me.

Then you hit me, why?
Punching and pushing me
Into the dark corner of our room.
Did you think it would make everything better?
You slid down the wall beside me
Crying,
I knew then that this was the end.

Laura Foster (14)
Ridgeway School

THE UNIVERSE

I look up in the sky at night, I see the universe,
Infinite, like a large cloak, worn by a god,
Patterned with sequins.
Never-ending like a bowl of ice cream that refills itself,
Always a marvellous feeling when I see the universe.
As colourful as a treasure chest full of Spanish doubloons
That is every pirate's dream.

The stars are quite another thing,
They are small like our planet yet so bright,
Like pinpricks and sequins in a basket.
Makes me feel so insignificant,
Like a broken doll,
I love to look up in the sky and see the universe.

One day I want to be an astronaut,
And fly to Jupiter, Saturn, Mars,
I will be the first human to visit all the planets,
And even further beyond.
Who knows what wondrous planets wait to be explored
Out in the universe
So far, we've only touched the surface.

Paul Hunt (11)
Ridgeway School

KUBLAI KHAN

As the sun beams,
Over bridges, over streams.
A great red dragon stands,
In front of the playing bands.

Loads of plants and flowers,
With great trees like towers.
Water flows over fountains,
Like great overflowing mountains.

Inside are sparkling marble floors,
As you walk through great oak doors.
Curtains made of bright red silk,
The whole room smells of milk.

Seats made of solid gold,
In the winter were very cold.
As I fell out the door,
I woke up and dreamt no more.

Sarah Becs (13)
Ridgeway School

KUBLAI KHAN

As you enter the wonderful palace of Kublai Khan,
You see all the golden pillars and colourful plants,
You hear the quiet trickling of the fountains
And the patter of the servants' feet as they rush across the floor,
Preparing the magnificent feast before the king enters the door.
The great Kublai Khan parades,
With fireworks, colourful clothes and banners, which are handmade.
You hear the quiet little conversations of the children who are
                                        playing games.
You watch and wonder who this marvellous emperor is.
There are statues of him all over this place,
There are tigers in the fields, roaming all over the land.
As you leave the palace gates and look at the stern guards,
They have decorated swords, which really do look grand,
As you think of all the statues, you think back to Kublai Khan,
You think, he must be grand,
But the answer to your question still lies in your hands.

Abi Pyatt (13)
Ridgeway School

SADNESS

He who puts a smile on your face,
In which your eyes deny.
He who slinks in slyly,
And leaves you feeling empty inside.
And who's to say it will be all right in the end?
And who knows when it will all stop?
As cold and darkness is what he intends.

He who only gives you pain and despair,
But leaves you feeling trapped inside yourself,
And damaged beyond repair.
But just as sharply he comes, he goes,
Pouring out from inside yourself,
Leaving you to turn a new leaf,
Ready to strike again
With pain and grief.

Michael Stanton (13)
Ridgeway School

SCARED

I'm scared in the dark;
Walking in the park.
Wanting to be home;
Scared of being alone.

Scared of going to sleep;
Fed up with counting sheep.
I'm sweating in my bed;
Scared of the monsters in my head.

Now I'm scared of being woken;
Until the voices have spoken.
Are the voices in my dream?
Or is it my mum I can hear scream?

Billy Heale (13)
Ridgeway School

MY BIKE

My bike
Is very special to me,
Brilliant, bouncy, cool,
As clean as my dad's car,
As good as a Marin,
Makes me feel rich,
Half as rich as David Beckham,
My bike,
Reminds me of how lucky I am,
Makes me think of Martyn Ashton,

Down at the dirt ramps and Plymco too,
I do jumps and wheelies, always fall off,
Endows and bunny hops, always fall off,
Always in the air,
Makes me feel like a pro,
I'm crazy for my age,
As the older boys say,
So best I calm down,
Do some other hobbies apart from football and biking,
Try basketball and even cricket too.

Darren Franklin (11)
Ridgeway School

INFANT ON THE TARN'S EDGE

This love is binding
Almost blinding
Although I'm still no further in finding
My lost soul which lies within.

Still in my caring
I'm always sharing
My heart which seems so duty bearing
My lost soul which lies within.

Like a white hot poker
Or a choking choker
This love is the thought-provoker
Of my soul which lies within.

Dreams of my path to golden glory gripping
While in front of me, my meagre life is ripping
And the dark tarn in which my virgin toes are dipping
That's where my lost soul lies within.

Jessica Pike (14)
Ridgeway School

KUBLAI KHAN

A world of beauty and wealth,
With patterns and colour.
Music fit for the King's ears,
Dancing fit for the Queen's eyes.
A world of beauty and wealth.

There he was in his land,
That Kublai Khan they call him.
His palace of ice, gold and riches.
Was someone trying to warn him?
In case it all goes wrong.

It's only a dream,
Only a dream I say,
A dazed dream,
What can possibly go wrong?
He could lose his riches, maybe.

This person's trying to tell him,
Warn him, frighten him.
What is he trying to tell him?
What can possibly go wrong?

Nikki Bredin (13)
Ridgeway School

TEENAGE DIRTBAG

Smelly socks everywhere,
Smelly, dirty underwear.
Pigsty rooms, scruffy hair
What they look, like they don't care!
Untidy clothes, lazy bum
What lives in their drawers, their tidy mum!
Greasy hair, big red zits
When you see them, you'd end up in laughing fits!
Teenage dirtbag laying on the bed
Surrounded by comics they've read and read
Always grumpy, in a mood
Always stuffing their face with food
When you're near them you'll need gas masks
'Cause they've never even heard of taking baths!
The only trouble is I'm talking about me and my friends!

Melanie Standlick (13)
Ridgeway School

THE PLAYGROUND

Take the children to the playground
Hear them laugh, watch them run
Enter through the gate, the fun has just begun.

Playing on the roundabout
Laughing in the sun
All the children laugh and shout
Young ones having fun
Giving pushes on the swing
Running round and round
On and off the other things
Up and over, up and down
Now the sky is getting dark
Day is over, time to leave the park.

Jamie Armstrong (12)
Ridgeway School

LOVE AND HATE

Love is a very precious thing,
Joy and happiness is what it brings,
It is with you every day and night,
It is like an everlasting light.
Hate is a devil's curse,
Which when you are affected you must reverse,
It can tear you apart without you knowing,
Because otherwise the tears will start flowing.

Sarah Love (13)
Ridgeway School

COURAGE AND COWARDICE

Courage is standing up to your fears,
Cowardice is making people shed tears,
Do you get bullied at school?
Or do you face up to them?
Is it scary when they walk up to you?
Do they think they're cool?
You should not fear them.
They are cowards themselves.
Picking on people younger than them,
Just ignore them.
They are no sorts of friends.

Michael Hagan (12)
Ridgeway School

RISK OF LOVE

Broken hearts are all we're leaving behind
What we're losing doesn't matter
It's what we're going to see in the future
By staying apart we're missing out on a good time
So let's get together before it's too late
Because I want you bad and I want you now

Broken hearts, let's leave it all in the past
Let's get together now
Let's get together fast

Carly McIntosh (13)
Ridgeway School

GARAGE NUMBER 17

Dark and damp and the stench of petrol,
Not the kind of place you'd expect to start a relationship.
But what if it was a secret relationship filled with guilt and betrayal.

Talking. Just talking. Harmless.
But what if it develops into something you can't ignore.
A forbidden love.

You have to talk, you have to tell someone.
Someone who will understand,
But you can't, you can't breathe a word of it to anyone.

You know it's wrong, but you carry on regardless.
You have to satisfy the burning desire.
It makes you so guilty that you feel sick inside.

You have to stop before someone gets hurt,
Even then the truth could still get out.
But the memories will always remain,
From garage number 17.

Elizabeth Shaw (14)
Ridgeway School

MY PARENTS

Mum and Dad are getting older
Should I help out more,
I do ¼ of the housework
The rest is done by Mum.

I buy my own clothes and make-up
So Mum and Dad don't pay
We're short of money as it is,
So why do they say we're okay.

They try and make life fun
They let us do what we want
They take us on holiday all the time
And won't do much for themselves.

Soon they won't have time,
So why don't they do things now
They really confuse me at times
But I'm glad that they're my parents.

Amy Barrowdale (14)
Ridgeway School

I DON'T GET OLD AGE

I don't get old age
I don't get old age
The way people wrinkle
Like a 3 week old plum
The way they get grey hair
It just doesn't make sense
They commence as smooth as soup
And depart like shrivelled shrimps
What makes them change
Is it stress or just their choice?

I don't get old age
I don't get old age
The way they lose their memory
The way they lose their hearing
Do they misplace it
Or do they do it for attention?
I just don't get old age
How about you?

Ashley Morrison (13)
Ridgeway School

KUBLAI KHAN

My head drifting away
Down a sinuous rill
Cedars athwart the chasm
Did I take that pill?

Singers out a loud
Dancers a proud
Creating a crowd
Costumes bright
As the night
Opens a cheerful
Bright night
Has begun
Did I take that pill?

The lawn long and green
Created by no machine
Golden pleasure domes
Unimaginable to man
The grand ice caves
Demanded by Kublai Khan
An area of exotic fruits
Men with golden boots

Acrobats performing
To a crowd so large
Dragon boats large and long
Peacefully drifting on

Diamonds encrusted
Rubies red and round
All for a man
Lucky enough to afford

The palace is grand
Silk at every window
Fish in the hall
Not of any sort
They are for a man
That can afford a golden roof

There are red ones
Green ones
Blue ones
And orange
Pink ones
Grey ones
And yellow.
All for a man
That can afford a golden roof
That paradise land
Sticks in my mind
Nice and easy to find.

William Amery (13)
Ridgeway School

LOVE AND HATE

Hate is something nobody wants,
Love is something everyone needs,
Hate is stupid, it gets you nowhere,
Love brings people together,
It makes the world a better place;
Hate causes violence, it brings you strife,
Love causes friendship, it brings you peace,
Hate takes away all your confidence,
But love is best by far.

Jade Follett (12)
Ridgeway School

KUBLAI KHAN

I enter a world of colour, a place with mystery
A palace made of crystal, glass and jade statues.
I see people, artists and then Kublai Khan.
Tiger skins spread on luxury bedroom floors.
Pictures of dragons signed in Chinese symbols.

I hear the sound of water trickling over a small waterfall.
The smell of food, the smell of flowers,
The scent of incense burning in the distance.
People shouting, hunting for animals for food, for rugs.

The laughter coming from people, the happiness.
I look to my left, I see fields full of colour;
I look to my right, I see people working,
Producing good things for the Kublai Khan.
I saw Kublai Khan, he turned away.
A bright light shone brightly, wiping my vision completely.
I had woken, woken to realise it was a dream, just a simple dream.

Amy Lane (14)
Ridgeway School

OUTER SPACE

Sometimes I dream about outer space,
And pretend I'm really there,
I wander around in my favourite place
And meet aliens covered in hair!

I fly around in my space rocket,
Drifting all around,
With mini aliens that fit in pockets,
Never making a sound.

I go exploring on Mars and Venus,
Where there're loads of pubs,
Aliens that love to please us
And unfortunately loads of thugs!

But when I wake up in the early day,
Thinking what went on in my head,
Then my mum will come in and say,
'Get up and out of that bed!'

Bethany Bailey (12)
Ridgeway School

KUBLAI KHAN

As I walk around,
My head is spinning,
All I can see is gold and riches,
It's more beautiful than you can imagine,
Fountains, rivers, statues and fireworks,
Kublai is overpowering,
The Palace
It has silks, rugs and even guards,
It's hot, dry and dusty,
But I love it.
I wish I could stay,
For the Chinese New Year,
I've heard all about it,
Kite fights and dragons,
I just wish I could stay,
And be part of their culture,
With panda skins, hats and karate.

Adam Steele (13)
Ridgeway School

LIBRARY LOUDNESS

'Excuse me do you have . . .'
'Eh . . . what, speak up boy.'
'I said do you have a . . .'
'What? I'm a tad bit deaf'
'Well I said do . . .'
'OK, now say it nice and loud,
But not too loud we're in a library'
'Excuse me do . . .'
'Oww, my ears, what are you doing shouting in the library,'
'I'm going to have to ask you to leave.'
'But . . .'

Matthew Moore (11)
Ridgeway School

FOOTBALL

I love it when we're winning
And hate it when we lose.
We always play out hardest
And I often get a bruise.
We have a celebration
But sometimes a confrontation.
Football is great
I play with my mates
And nothing can compare.

Matthew Rogers (11)
Ridgeway School

KUBLAI KHAN

I drifted off into a drugged dream.
I awake with the sound of a gentle
Flowing stream in the garden of a palace.
I see lots of beautiful concubines
All around me.
I was dressed in tiger skins and gold jewellery.
I have servants waiting on me.
There's statues of tigers and elephants made of marble and jade.
Stone pillars at the entrance of the palace.
As I clap my hands three concubines come over
holding mirrors and fans.
I clap my hands again and a concubine comes over.
I wake up and the amazing dream is over.

Lee Chittenden (14)
Ridgeway School

AFTER CHRISTMAS

Take the tree and decorations down
Throw away the wrapping paper,
All ripped up and torn,
Do washing and ironing what people have worn,
Wiping dishes and glasses clean,
Hoover where the tree has been,
Put all presents in a stack,
Hoping, dreaming Santa comes back!

Natalie Jackson (11)
Ridgeway School

MY DOGS

My dogs are golden,
black and white.
The white glows through
on a moonlit night.
When the sun rises from
the hills, over land and
over mills,
they know what they have to
do to see the boring day through.

They are there to greet us
after a hard working day.
Summer, spring and autumn
mostly in May.
They are wary of strangers
and they protect the house,
they would even growl
at the smallest mouse.
They are mostly there to cheer
us up when we are very sad.

We are their family
they protect us in the evening
and watch us through the night.
They always care for us with their big hearts.
Their love is always in different parts.
Some people say they are mad
but they are there to cheer us up
when we are very sad.
All I can say is they are the best dogs in the world.

Helen Maloney (11)
Ridgeway School

LOVE POEMS

Not a box of chocs or a kissagram

I give you a lemon
It is the calm after the storm
It promises tranquillity
Like the beginning of the stream.

Take it
It will blind you with sourness
Like a jealous partner.
It will make your mouth
Tingle like a kiss.

I'm not trying to be sweet

No need for satin sheets.

I give you a lemon
Its flavour will stay in your mouth
Truthful and forgiveful
As we are
As long as we are.

Here.
Its care is like an hourglass
To show how long we have left
If you want.
Deadly
Its sweet deceptive smell will tempt you
To its sharp, sour centre.

Thomas Smith (14)
Ridgeway School

IF YOU WERE GONE

If you were gone
There would be no sound. Silence.
My eyes would melt into quiet blue pools
And any words would be washed away
With the rain that is my tears.

If you were gone
I would be lifeless
I would struggle to breathe
My body would ache
And my heart would hang half mast.

If you were gone
My mind would freeze over
And my own thoughts would fade.
Your picture would be printed onto my mind
Never to be erased.

If you were gone
The heavens would open
The rain would crash down
The lightning would blind me
And the thunder would penetrate my thoughts.

But for now you're still here
And I'll hold you close
Breathing in the scent of your subtle perfume
Clinging to you forever,
I'll never let go.
But, I wanted you to know
What I would do
If you were gone.

If you were gone.

Sara Gaydon (15)
Ridgeway School

KUBLAI KHAN

Pretty views from the open window,
Fragrant smells from the flowers,
Sparkling water, gleaming in the sunlight,
The meandering rivers,
Statues of ancestors, surrounded by stones,
Tiles around, made of marble,
Excitable festivals to celebrate the seasons,
Kites floating high above,
Chinese dragon boats floating on the rivers,
The rows of perfect flowers,
The towers standing tall and wide,
Chinese banners everywhere,
The rooms in the tower, long and wide,
The rooms in the palace, rich in colours,
The rooms, made of stone and marble,
The staircase, with a golden handrail,
The beds are made of silk,
The kitchen, with rushing servants,
Dining rooms, mostly made from oak and pine,
Then I hear the whispering, from the thoughts in my head,
I can't quite describe them,
I listen again,
They are getting louder, warning me about war,
Telling me to be ready,
Ready for what? I think,
One day there could be a big war and I could lose everything,
But I don't want to do that,
I could never imagine what it would be like,
Where would I go?
What would I do, and who would I turn to?

Jessica Baskott (13)
Ridgeway School

MAKE ME THE BEST SKATEBOARDER IN THE WORLD

Into a boiling pot of greased lightning,
Add one skateboard deck,
Sprinkle on one hair of Tony Hawk,
Then drizzle in the sweat of Chad Muska.
Roast a skateboard
Mix in the fastest wheels in the world,
And burnish with stickers
Toast the trainers of Steve Caballero
With the shirt of Bob Burnquest
Heat the mixture to the speed of light
And pour into Burntwist cups
Stir in Abec 7 bearings
And serve in a mini half-pipe
And then you have yourself a kickfliptabulous
To make me the best skateboarder
In the world!

Anthony Boulton (12)
Ridgeway School

KUBLAI KHAN

As I drift off into my drugged dream
I wake with the sound of a gently flowing stream
I realise now I can see
I'm in the palace of Kublai Khan
The palace where reality and dreams merge
Where fact and fiction are the same thing
I see marble, jade, gold, glass and tiger skins
Servants waiting on me
Stone pillars surround the palace on every side
I drifted off with the sound of the steam
As I awake from my enchanted dream.

Shaun Vinecombe (14)
Ridgeway School

FIVE FOOT THREE

Marry, marry, if only I could,
But only a teenager and so in love,
She's blonde, she's tall,
Unlike me,
For I'm too small for her to see!

If only she would smile and look my way,
The courage I would have to turn and say,
Your eyes are shiny and oh so blue,
And if I could I would marry you!
She's blonde, she's tall,
Unlike me,
For I'm too small for her to see!

I dawdle along her street each day,
But still she doesn't look my way,
Dragon to slay, a mountain to climb,
I only hope I have the time,
She's blonde, she's tall,
Unlike me,
For I'm too small for her to see!

People stop to say hello,
How sad I feel they'll never know
A pat on the back I often get,
Never mind there's time to grow yet
She's blonde, she's tall,
Unlike me,
For in reality I'm but
Five foot three.

Nicholas Hunt (14)
Ridgeway School

KUBLAI KHAN

The walls filled with beautiful flowers.
All the flower beds planted perfectly.
And as you enter the palace,
Everything looks too fragile to touch.
Even all the servants are dressed immaculately.
It is a floaty, dreamy place.
Every little detail takes your breath away.
The scenery from every corner is amazing.
All the wall hangings, sewn to perfection.
Every single human that works there,
Walks to perfection.
The palace must be made up of a hundred bedrooms.
More than the whole of our classes put together.
The food looks too good to eat,
As it is laid out on the precious silk tablecloth.
As all the people sit down to eat,
They choose from a variety of cutlery,
All gold and sparkling, from the beautiful sunlight.
The windows let in a cool breeze,
Which lets the curtains flow with the wind.
But, before they eat,
The enormous, carved wooden doors open,
And in walks Kublai Khan.
He sits on his throne encrusted with rich jewels,
The sun beating down on his head.

Helen Jory (14)
Ridgeway School

WHEN I'M OLD

I am old and I live by myself,
Eat and drink by myself,
Collect my pension by myself,
And do my shopping by myself.

I am 72, my wife has died,
I miss her so, I cried and cried.
My dear children have children of their own,
I wish that they would come back home.

Lawrence Turlej (13)
Ridgeway School

LOVE DOESN'T FRIGHTEN ME!

Hearts in the hall
Writing on the wall
Love doesn't frighten me
Kisses on the cheek
Hugs through the week
Love doesn't frighten me.

Bouquets of flowers
Talking at all hours
Love doesn't frighten me
Walking hand in hand
Across the silky sand
Love doesn't frighten me.

Chocolates and hearts
Let's never be apart
Love doesn't frighten me
Candlelit dinner for two
When I say I do
Love doesn't frighten me.

Children and marriage
Honeymoon in a carriage
Love frightens me
Love really frightens me.

Hannah Dolan (14)
Ridgeway School

KUBLAI KHAN

Falling asleep, deep asleep
Twisting and turning in your deep, deep sleep
Open your eyes in the land of doze
The colours and smells of Kublai Khan
He is standing on the doorstep of a beautiful palace
Gardens ten miles round, and full of joy and gladness
Singers and dancers full of joy inside
The towering domes of the palace behind

Gardens of colour
Gardens of smells
With a beautiful stream trickling down
Statues of people and statues of him
Statues of everything not boring or dim

The palace inside is a beautiful place
Curtains of silk and golden lace
A fountain of water in the most beautiful place
A four-poster bed hung with silk and lace
Robes of reds and tiger skins lay
The bed looks comfy so I will lie
But then I woke up and I had fled
I was in my very own bed.

Deborah D'Arcy (14)
Ridgeway School

EXTREME

Extreme can be good
Extreme can be bad
Extreme can make you happy
Extreme can make you sad.

Kyle Clarke (11)
Ridgeway School

KUBLAI KHAN

He lies there on his silky bed
Servants feeding him grapes
Statues of gold and silver stand in
the beauty of the palace
Tiger cubs lounge in the shade of the tropical trees
Pandas sit there munching on their sugar cane
Singers and dancers lie on the
river bed rehearsing lines for the show tonight
As birds fly in the sun's gleam
Tiger skins grace the floor and bed of Kublai
He sits on his marbled throne with silk cushions
He looks like a powerful man but acts like a normal man
He has the power over millions of people
He does what he wants when he wants
and no one can say no to him
His palace of reality is another's dream.

Liam Brett (14)
Ridgeway School

EIFFEL TOWER

The Eiffel Tower
Made of metal
Towering, gigantic made from manpower.
Like a huge pole of metal coming out the ground
Like a capital A
It will astound.
Makes me feel like an ant
The Eiffel Tower
How small humans are in the world.

Joe Higson (11)
Ridgeway School

KUBLAI KHAN

Dreary, dreary
Falling into a drugged snooze.
Drowsy, drowsy
Drifting between reality and a dreamy world.
Dreamy, dream
Floating into the world of Kublai Khan.

Towering domes adorned with banners.
Pillars entwined with Chinese dragons
And artists painting pictures of dragon talons.
And there, standing at the foot of the hill, Kublai Khan!
The son of Ogedei Khan!

Meanwhile, in the centre of the pleasure dome,
There was all manner of music and dance.
Dulcimers played and slave girls roamed
Delivering feasts with a choreographed prance.

This is the world of Kublai Khan
A very kind and gracious man!

Dreary, dreary,
Out and away from the world of the pleasure dome.
Drowsy, drowsy,
Out of the world of the beautiful palace.
Dreamy, dreamy,
Out of the world of Kublai Khan!

Shaun Jackson (14)
Ridgeway School

KUBLAI KHAN

As I enter the wonderful palace of Kublai Khan
I see the magnificent pillars of gold, sparkling in the sun.
The wonderful water fountains with lotuses catch my eye.
As I walk into the garden, I see land stretched out for ten miles.
With domes, caves, dancers and musicians.
With rivers meandering over the fertile land,
I see the wonderful parades of Kublai Khan,
With wealth and colour,
Laughing and dancing, with sumptuous feast,
All the troubles are distant.
As I enter the palace once again,
I see this mighty emperor,
Oh, isn't he pleasing to the eye?

He goes into a rage, demanding to know who I am,
He calls upon the guards,
And they drag me away and take me to the prison,
I fall upon the bed.
As I listen to the peaceful singing,
I gradually fall asleep.

And that is when I awake,
Snuggled up in my comfortable chair,
With the sun gleaming on my face,
A book on my lap, reading,
The travels in ancient China, in the time of the great emperor,
Kublai Khan.

Fawn Bennetts (13)
Ridgeway School

THE OLD MAN I WILL BE

When I am old I shall dye what's left of my hair green
Like grass
And wear a top hat with the price tag left in.
I'll have a luminous yellow Mini,
That doesn't work properly and I'll hog the road.
I'll take out my teeth, to scare my young grandchildren
Like an old Dracula.
I'll play pranks on people, tell rude jokes and make
Flatulent noises.
I'll hum out of tune and whistle a lot
Like a deaf bird.
When I am old you'd better beware because I could just
Be around the corner waiting,
Waiting to play a prank on you.

Richard Vinecombe (13)
Ridgeway School

KUBLAI KHAN

Marble pillars tower the sky; I wish that I were there
The sweet smell of strawberries linger everywhere
Sweet-smelling roses as red as blood
Beautiful waterfalls glitter in the sunlight
Beautiful musicians playing peaceful tunes
Butterflies fluttering in the sky
I wish I was a part of this beautiful kingdom but I'm not,
Why?

Rebecca Mina (14)
Ridgeway School

KUBLAI KHAN

The glory of the palace
Built on Xanadu
Kublai's story shocked the world
All the way to Kathmandu
His palace big
And very strong
Some people thought
It was very wrong
But didn't say a word
For they feared for their lives
And their sons, daughters
And even their wives
There were tiger skins, panda skins
Servants of many
Marble walls, tiled floors
Concubines so many!
His murderous grandfather Genghis
A Mongolian warrior too
Shocked the world as much
As the palace in Xanadu
Food his was great
His food was fine
His servants were scared
His wine was divine
Kublai and his story
Lived on for thousands of years
His empire, his palace and concubines
But people have no fear
For he is dead.

Danny Harris (15)
Ridgeway School

KUBLAI KHAN

A dazed dream, was it true?
Was I in the Khan's palace?
The one he ordered so many years ago.
I pinched myself until my skin turned red sore
My chin fell to the ground
All the wondrous books I had read,
They could not make up for the feeling I was experiencing now.

The glare of the sun as it reflected in the mountain of gold
that was his palace,
As I reached the oak doors my heart was pounding
with nerves and anticipation.
As I opened it, the creaking drowned out the hustle and bustle
of the nearby market,
My feet tapped to the sound of the bellowing drum.

I was inside, this golden splendour
Wall to wall of jewels and velvet.
And spread along the marble floor,
A carpet of tiger skins.
A never-ending hall scented with incense
As I inched closer to the partly opened door,
The smell of oriental spices and dishes drifted through.

I pushed open the door and peeped in,
It was the garden.
Every colour you can imagine was all in this wondrous place,
Mountains of rainbow colour, and sinuous rills,
Running down and around and over the hills,
Rivers of honey and fountains of gold,
Stories of war whispered in secret,
As the Khan sat proud on his palanquin.

This world had seemed so real to me,
But as I woke to find it was a dream,
Or was it, was it real?
Or somewhere I thought I'd been?

Michelle Kendall (14)
Ridgeway School

KUBLAI KHAN

I dream of,
Gardens stretching for miles on end,
The rivers and fountains vibrating,
Marble stairs meandering upwards,
Fur rugs and throws everywhere in sight.
Suddenly, a man in the distance,
A rich man approaching in fine silks.
Could it possibly be Kublai Khan
Heading towards me on horseback?
He entered and tied up the horse.
I can't believe it, I can't believe it,
It's Kublai Khan, it's Kublai Khan.

I dream of,
Him standing there in fine woven silk clothes,
Ceramics and china everywhere,
Servants and butlers rushing around,
Lots of people all dressed in fine clothes,
Me just standing there in my nightclothes,
Everyone else in ball gowns.
How stupid I felt, so underdressed,
I wanted to escape from the dome,
I roamed around the peaceful gardens,
Then I found myself lying in my bed,
I had dreamed of Kublai Khan.

Natasha Garrad (14)
Ridgeway School

THE WAR

Happiness hangs silent upon the air,
Like a spider's silken thread waiting to ensnare,
Misery as it seeks to hold man's weak soul,
On its first ever day of life.

Sadness is also waiting, to grab its first victim,
As he too hangs silently above, unnoticed
By mere mortals, who live their lives
By the struggles for worldly goods,
Too ignorant to realise that.

Happiness is always there to hold your hand,
When an army of sadness drifts across the land.

Annette Goddard (12)
Ridgeway School

KUBLAI KHAN

As I drift into the world of sleep,
I see statues of marble, glass and jade.
Music plays, dangers glide and singers chant in the sun
As it glistens off the glass domes.
Servants scuffle around delivering food for feasts.
Birds chirp a fine tune as they rest on the palace roof.
Kublai Khan rests in his chair of glistening gold
radiating the sun.
The music gets louder and louder.
I feel drowsy, slipping away from the world of Kublai Khan.

Stuart MacManus (14)
Ridgeway School

KUBLAI KHAN

I awake in a calm and peaceful place.
As my eyes open, everything is still.
No wind is blowing and no rain is dropping.
The sky is clear, no white puffy shapes to be seen.

As I look around I see great gardens of beauty and tranquillity,
Two big domes that seem to be full of luxurious flowers.
At the end of the garden, there stood the magnificent palace,
Many steps to walk up, but looked worth it.

The palace glittered in the sun and looked as good as new.
Six beautiful pillars stood at the front of the palace,
Each with a different statue of Kublai Khan in front.
My favourite stood right in the middle.
The dark colour of jade changed shades in the sun.

I began to walk around the magnificent garden, but then,
A richly coloured palanquin stopped me.
Covered in silk and golden framework,
Rich shades of purple, blue, green and red.

As it passed me, it stopped,
Then there in front of me stood the great Kublai Khan.
I looked him straight in the eye.
His smile looked so false.
Did he enjoy this style of life or just put on a brave face?

I walked towards him, but as I did he vanished.
Everything was beginning to disappear.
Then I awoke in my warm bed.
It was just a dream.

Kelly Temlett (14)
Ridgeway School

KUBLAI KHAN

The river meandering down to the ocean,
Cedars and smells of fresh flowers all around,
The atmosphere was in slow motion,
While watching doves fly through the air and making their sounds,
The clear blue skies,
The cool breeze on your face,
See the butterflies like coloured leaves falling from the skies,
Making this a wonderful place.

As I enter the dome, I hear dulcimer sounds,
I see people laughing, dancing or singing,
As I look around I see amazing things that I have found,
Forty white stone statues, and the stone walls,
Jade tiger statues - carved in a picture of a tiger's head,
Then all of a sudden music stops, the atmosphere is dead,
Enter Kublai Khan - the emperor of China,
I must leave this magical place, and fear for my life,
As rumours are mentioned there would be war one day.

Vicky Bawler (14)
Ridgeway School

KUBLAI KHAN

As I walk into the peaceful garden,
All I hear is music, lovely music.
Dancing girls dancing all around me,
Peaceful music playing to their dance.

I walked into the dome-like palace,
With its walls so tall and pillars of marble,
All I saw were statues,
Statues of Chinese dragons and people all around.

I took a step closer and heard a voice, I looked,
It was Kublai, Kublai Khan,
I couldn't believe my eyes.
He sat in front of a beautiful fountain,
With its glittering water running so fast.

I slowly walked through a big door,
Into a place full of food,
Strawberries, cherries, all the fruit you could think of,
Meat, vegetables and a sweet smell of roses.

Katie Smith (14)
Ridgeway School

KUBLAI KHAN

As I drift off into Kublai's world I see him covered in gold,
it's shining so brightly it almost blinds me.
There are hundreds of servants standing around him,
as if waiting to be asked for something.
Then the great emperor speaks.
His voice as soft as music but I could not understand
for he was speaking another language.
I then start to feel tired and the lush green grass
looks as soft as carpet.
I lie down and drift off slowly, slowly . . .
until everything is silent.
I awake to discover myself as the great emperor
with people surrounding me.
I remember the heat burning constantly.
I ask for a drink but it doesn't arrive.
I wake up in a cold sweat.
I then drift off slowly, slowly . . .

Ashley McKenna (14)
Ridgeway School

A MOROCCO DAY

An irresistible golden flare burning through
the ever-increasing fingers of light,
Stretching towards us as we sleep.
Dawn has broken.

A mysterious haze enveloping the mountains
that tower over us like sleeping giants in the midday heat.

Faces of sweet anticipation
as we walk through the busy marketplace.
Filled with the overwhelming aroma of herbs and spices.
Our ears pounding by the sound of delight,
as we enter the world of street merchants and their families.

The day comes to an end as the sky begins to burn flamboyantly
swallowing the last rays of light,
as we say goodnight.

Jennifer Kelly (15)
Ridgeway School

EVIL, GOOD

As cold hands grasp me tightly,
A surge of anger boils my blood.
I reach for any weapon,
This is *evil* in its strongest form.

I smash a window,
I break a door,
What am I doing all this for?
It's all the evil burning inside me,
Taking control of mind and body.

The hands loosen their painful grip,
The blood is flowing calmly now.
I throw the weapon to the floor
And sit upon the chair.

I look around at my destruction,
My evil is trailing away.
The fire in my heart is extinguished,
I control myself once again.

Jonathan Dodds (12)
Ridgeway School

A HIP HOP OLD MAN

When I am older I'm gonn   a be a DJ
a groovy old man you see

With race cars, money and
brunettes up to my knees

I'm gonna be the next Ali G
a wicked old man you see!

With jet planes and choppers

I'm gonna be a model
a gorgeous old man you see

With gold and silver bikes

When I'm older I'm gonna be a pensioner
an ugly old man you see

What do you think you will be?

Mathew Elson (14)
Ridgeway School

THE TWIN TOWERS

The terrorists came with evil in their eyes,
And anger in their minds,
They didn't care who they would kill,
And now the Twin Towers have been stabbed
And have fallen.
The dust arises with souls of the dead,
The families are crying,
And the enemy rejoicing,
And now they're trying to find the killer,
But with no hope.
They'll have to admit the good are fair,
And the bad are evil.

Daniel Wadman (12)
Ridgeway School

GREAT GRANDAD

His voice is like a big bass drum
He is a bag of spuds
He gulps his tea like a black hole
He is built like a wall
His eyes are like a raging river
His ears are like two satellite dishes
He is very untidy
He smells like freshly ploughed earth
His hair is like freshly whipped cream
His nose is like bat's ears
His an odious giant
His feet are size 1000.

Ben Challen (13)
Ridgeway School

MY DOG GUINNESS

My dog Guinness
Is the family pet
He's as black as the night
Also as cuddly as a teddy bear
And as sweet as sugar

My dog Guinness
Is the family pet
He likes it when you playfight
Only if you fight fair
But he's still a little fatty
Who doesn't like to share

My dog Guinness
Is the family pet
He likes to walk and run
He loves it on the beach
And also in the sun.

Kirsty Agnew (11)
Ridgeway School

EVIL IS A SIN

Evil grabs you in your youth
Completely rids you of the truth
If you are evil you will find
You have no feelings and can't be kind
Makes you kill and commit sins
It ruins your life from deep within.

Kimberly Lewis (12)
Ridgeway School

AUTUMN

Autumn is here
The leaves start to fall
It starts to get cold
The birds start to call.

Winter is coming
It's getting too cold
We wear our hats
Because we are told.

Spring is here
We have some warm days
The flowers come out
And children start to play.

Summer has arrived
It's getting too hot
We jump in our pools
And cool ourselves down.

Rebecca Knight (11)
Ridgeway School

FEELINGS

Happiness is like the wind through the trees,
But when you pass away the trees don't move.
Sadness is like having no way to turn,
But when you're found you could turn left or right.
Hate can be stubborn but also fair,
Love can be free as air but also as tight as a knot.
Be fair like free air, not as stubborn as the bear.

Kirsty Barnett (12)
Ridgeway School

In The Playground

Out in the playground where I play with my friends
I play on the monkey bars and the swing on the trees
I sometimes go to the canteen for a bite to eat
I enjoy playing football and other sports
I sometimes just hang out with my friends

We play lots of games
We enjoy eating in the canteen
We enjoy hanging around
We even enjoy just playing about
And we don't like it when break is over

When I go to the library I want to read a book
When I go to the sports hall I like to play some sport
When I play a game I like to play a game I like
When we play it is really great
When the bell rings there goes break!

Matthew Thornton (11)
Ridgeway School

Life . . .

Sadness is beautiful in its own way,
Yet loneliness is tragic, forever day by day.
But once upon a lifetime,
When you find someone who's there day and night,
Who sets your loneliness free and makes your life so bright,
Forget the past, it's history,
And let the future lead you into a mystery.

Laura Proctor (12)
Ridgeway School

STUDENTS AND TEACHERS

S   illy behaviour
T   roublemakers
U   seless
D   unce's hat
E   quals 10+2
N   aughty
T   roublesome
S   tudents

T   elling you off
E   leven+three=fourteen
A   rt teacher
C   aught you talking
H   istory teacher
E   ating in his class
R   eligious studies
S   cience teacher
        Aaahhh!
        All those teachers!

Kelly Vinecombe (12)
Ridgeway School

MAGIC

Magic is the source of dreams,
Mystery in a book,
Magical, fiery crystal ball,
Nightmares, never dare to look.
Flying kite of darkness,
Strong as a lightning bolt,
Master of the raging storm,
Chant our magic cult.

Emma Pike (12)
Ridgeway School

WHEN I GROW OLD

When I grow old I'm going to be active,
I'm not going to sit down all day long,
I'll wear Tammy Girl clothes,
And not Marks and Spencer clothes.

When I grow old I'll spend my money on other people,
So they will spend their money on me,
And they'll do me favours,
If I need them to or not.

When I grow old I'll invite family
And friends over to dinner,
Then sit down for a while
And watch things like Top of the Pops.

When I grow old I'll
Watch nature programmes like the ones I used to,
And all the latest pop concerts,
Not all of the soaps and war films.

When I grow old,
My grandchildren will call me Groovy Gran,
They will say to all the other children,
'My nan ain't normal, she's special,'
Then they will tell me what they did at school,
But that's when I'm old.

Kayleigh Ramsden (13)
Ridgeway School

OLD BUT FULL OF LIFE

When I'm old, I'm going to walk for miles
And I'll have loads of different funky hairstyles.
I'm going to run the marathon
Like teenagers at a fairground.
Then I'll sit in the pub and drink loads of pints,
And listen to the murmur and music in the background.
I'll have dogs for pets and I'll keep them well trained,
I'll feed them up with food but give more to my Great Dane.
My house will stand out in the street,
With purple walls, blue doors and a touch of orange spots.
I'll have people round to stay and eat,
If I don't get on with them, I'll give them to my dogs as meat.
In the mornings I'll jog for fun,
To see all the mums taking their kids to school.
Then I'll get on my motorbike and drive to the mall,
Spend all my pension on anything I like.
I'll enter competitions,
I'll win them all.
Then I'll come home to rest,
Play poker then fall asleep
On my blue, pink and yellow spotted sofa.

Becky Rixon (13)
Ridgeway School

DANGER AND SAFETY

Danger in the dark
When you're walking through the park
It's OK with your friends
But the danger never ends
My belief will carry me
It will never drop thee

I'm on my journey
While the opportunity
Passes by
To stay safe
As you walk through danger
And watch your life drift away.

Fraser Tarrant (12)
Ridgeway School

STRANGER

When I look in the mirror I see,
An old-looking woman looking back at me.
With once big blue eyes as big as the sea,
Now shrunk with time.
Looking so frail and old
Like a screwed up piece of paper.

When I look in the mirror I see
Thoughts and dreams dashed at the seams.
With only distant memories,
Once curled up at night
With thoughts in sight.

When I look in the mirror, what do I really see?
A young woman
With thoughts and dreams
Who waits with open arms for me.

When I look in the mirror I see,
An old stranger
Who was once young but now look at me.

Don't look and stare
Because you'll be looking in this mirror soon.

Sarah Rayne (13)
Ridgeway School

WHEN I GROW OLD I WANT TO BE . . .

When I grow old I want to see,
A hip hop granny looking back at me.
I want to have really hideous pink hair,
And run around giving people a scare.

I want to be free and have loads of fun,
And hopefully do all the things I wanted done.
I would like to be a teenage dirtbag baby,
And hopefully too have really bad rabies.

When I am old I want to jump out of an aeroplane,
I really don't want my life to be really, really tame.
I want to go around with a stereo to my ear,
And let all the teenagers shudder with fear.

I want to be a granny who is really quite hip,
Not to be moaning about my old knackered hip.
To go around and steal from the shops,
Because now it would not matter if I was caught by the cops.

When I am old I want to see,
A cool, funky granny looking back at me!
But what I don't want to see,
Is a lonely old woman looking back at me!

Andrea Smith (13)
Ridgeway School

HAIKU

Mondays are boring
Don't like school work in class
I don't want homework

PE is the best
I love PE every week
It is so good

It was my birthday
It was the best day ever
It was so good there

I had the best day
It was so good with my friend
Then I went back home.

Jayden Burton (12)
Ridgeway School

GROOVY GRAN

When I am old I shall have fun
Relaxing and enjoying the hot summer sun.
I shall go out shopping with my mate
And go back home really late.
I will have a house which is bright green
Which stands out and can be seen.
I'll have flowers in my garden, colourful and bright
People will say, 'What a beautiful sight!'
I will wear comfortable clothes which are pretty
They will make me feel happy and witty.
I shall have friends over for dinner
My splendid food is such a winner.
I may have a dog which I can take for a run
It will be like having a friend or a son.
I will be fit by going for a jog around the park
And I'll go out with my mates when it gets dark.
When I go out I will stay out really late
I'll be like a teenager when I'm out with my mate.
When I look in the mirror, what will I see?
A groovy old lady looking at me.
I'm a hip hop woman as you can see
That's what people say when they are looking at me.

Sarah Paull (13)
Ridgeway School

ISOLATION

Jews, Jews, Jews, Jews!
Nowhere to run, nowhere to hide,
Feeling sad and scared inside.

Soldiers, soldiers, soldiers, soldiers!
Demons from Hell, breathing flames,
Don't feel sorry and don't ask for names.

Camp, camp, camp, camp!
'People like vermin,' the soldiers say,
Tortured, slaughtered and killed every day.

Gas, gas, gas, gas!
Put in a room underground,
Everybody's watching, not a sound,
A man pushes a button wearing a gown.

Here comes the gas . . . I need to lie down . . .

Ryan Beasley (12)
Ridgeway School

HATRED OR KINDNESS?

Hatred engulfs you like a river overflowing,
Kindness is the sandbags that slow the torrents.
Hatred will turn you into a boiling kettle,
Only the coolness of kindness will calm you down.
Hatred is contagious, clouding people's minds,
Kindness eradicates the misty clouds.
Hatred will drive you mad,
Kindness is the only cure.

Daniel Gillings (12)
Ridgeway School

HARRY THE WORLD BOXING CHAMPION

Harry is a hamster
He admits that he's Italian
But people also know that
He's as tough as a black stallion

When he was an amateur
He used to mess about
But now that he's professional
He'd rather knock men out

In his first major match
He went against a frog
But he could beat him blindfolded
Whilst sitting on the bog

In the lightweight tournament
He hit men to the moon
No people are saying that
He will be the best soon

He had a love life too
But sadly he was gay
His boyfriend was a cat
Whose owners called him Jay

When he was a heavyweight
He went against the champ
But Harry sent him flying off
Without a postage stamp

He was challenged by a lion
Who could crush him in one stomp
When the match bell was sounded
Harry was eaten in one chomp.

Tom Barnes (13)
Ridgeway School

JEWS

I feel like a lost fish in the deep blue sea.
Constantly looking for my family.
I could be the next one to die.
The next rat in the snake pit.

Like a single star in the sky.
All alone and about to die.

The stench of blood fills the air.
I then look up and say a prayer.
I wonder if I'll escape or not,
Or be sent down in one clear shot.

I wish I was back at home,
Out in the yard playing with the garden gnome.

As I am about to inhale the gas,
I take a last look at the grass.
Then I have flashbacks of my home in Devon,
For I will meet my family up in Heaven.

Richard Weeks (12)
Ridgeway School

MY WISE GRAN

My wise gran,
Is brainy as anyone could be,
Bold, loving, delicate,
gShe could be on TV.

My wise gran,
Is exact and fine,
Kind, helpful, grand,
She isn't happy all the time.

My wise gran,
Is a beautiful lady,
Charming, dainty, elegant,
She is very brainy.

Danielle Watch (11)
Ridgeway School

LONELINESS

Loneliness . . .
What is loneliness?
Is it a disease?
Could it be contagious?
Is anyone immune?

Loneliness . . .
Boys, girls, men, women,
Young, old, short or tall;
No discrimination;
It knows no boundaries.

Loneliness . . .
Symptoms, are there any?
Total isolation.
Feeling so alone,
Even in a crowd.

Loneliness . . .
No one on the phone,
Shut off from the world.
Like a coiled spring uncurled,
No one should be so lonely.

Loneliness . . .
Why isn't there a cure?

Danielle McMullin (13)
Ridgeway School

ISOLATION OF THE JEWS

Isolation is the word you could use
To explain the life of the Jews.
Disease, gas chambers and torture,
There's really nothing to live for.
Like slaves being eaten away by rats,
And then to top it all, chased by cats.
There is no possible way of getting out,
You are bound to die, there's no doubt.
The guards treat you like scum
And that's really not fun.
You feel like a lonely rock in the bottomless sea
And know you will never be free.
I bet that you think there is no God,
Like a single pea in its tiny pod.

Kira Cartwright (12)
Ridgeway School

LOVE

Love is such a special thing,
It always makes my heartstrings ping.
Some days I'm happy, some I'm sad,
Love could never be that bad.
Love is when two people meet,
Love can knock you off your feet.
It can take you by surprise,
It's just a funfair ride.

Kylie Stonehouse (12)
Ridgeway School

GOOD AND EVIL

Good is like sitting on a cloud
Evil drowning on you to make you proud.
Good like Heaven
Evil like Hell.
Good things make you want to tell
Evil is like a demon
Horrible and dry
Good is like an angel
Beautiful and shy
Good is about the deeds you do
Evil is about . . .
That's for you to find out!

Sarah Barrow (12)
Ridgeway School

LOVE IS . . .

Love is a very special thing,
Love will take you under its wing,
Love can take you far and wide,
Love is like a magical ride,
Love is there when you need it most,
Your one true friend, life's only host,
Love will triumph over hate,
Even when you enter that pearly gate.

Carla Fice (12)
Ridgeway School

I LOVE FOOTBALL

I love it when we win,
I hate it when we lose,
We never let our guard down,
Unless we're on the booze.
I play it with my brothers,
I play it with my mates,
Nothing can compare with it,
Footie never waits.
I play it on the pitch,
I play it in the street,
I hope we never lose again,
Or else I'll be dead meat!

Justin Rule (12)
Ridgeway School

MY LITTLE FISH

My little fish,
Fat, pretty and dumb,
But she can be a little fun.
She swims around all day and night,
And then wakes up when she sees the light.
She swims away if I come too near,
Expecting me to disappear.
I hope one day that she will know,
That I will never hurt her so.

Katie Bennatto (11)
Ridgeway School

IN A JEW'S EYE

Why do they hate me?
I don't see what I've done wrong.
Is it the colour of my hair?
It's black, black as coal.
Do I wear different clothes?
Just jeans and T-shirt.
Jeans and T-shirt, like everybody else.
Or is it the house I live in?
It's brick and mortar, with a window and door,
Window and door just like any other.
Maybe it's because of my face,
It's not pretty, pretty like all the others.
I know
It's because I'm a Jew,
A Jew just like the rest of my family.

Jessica Fissler (12)
Ridgeway School

SPIDERS

Spiders,
They're creepy and crawly,
Big, small and scary,
Dangling from their long thin thread,
Like a puppet on a string,
As big as a tower
As small as a pea
Spiders
Creepy crawly scaring me.

Natasha Lane (11)
Ridgeway School

DEATH

You may be ignorant, you may be bright,
But death won't put up a fight.
It will draw you away like the years,
But to loved ones it'll cause tears.

Death will come in black and it's gnarled and fierce,
Your hearts and others it will pierce.
If you're rude or polite, no matter,
Death makes your emotions scatter.

And maybe to you this doesn't matter:
The Grim Reaper wants to natter.
It scares me to think that we are not safe:
For death can be all over the place.

It'll close up your life, bring it to an end,
But on your family you can depend.
Coming sudden maybe the case,
In front of you a deathly face.

Memories live on in mind,
Now eternal peace you will find.
You know in your heart you can't replace
That image of the deathly face.

Nicola Gaydon (13)
Ridgeway School

WHY DO I HAVE TO?

Why do I have to
Make cups of tea?
Make everybody's tea?
Go to bed at 9.00?
Brush my teeth?

Why do I have to
Always keep my room tidy?
Always do my best?
Why
Somebody please tell me?

Claire Geach (12)
Ridgeway School

PEPPER

My pet kitten
She is called Pepper
She is 5 months old
Pepper is very funny
Cute and loving
Pepper is just mine
And I love her
Very much
She is really naughty
But I don't care
I love her so much
She loves to play and bite
Her favourite food is rabbit

She also likes chicken
Pepper has got a long
Bushy tail
She is furry
And I think she is
Very naughty
When she is tired
She curls up in a ball.

Cherish Kendall (11)
Ridgeway School

ISOLATION

I felt like an island
In the middle of the ocean,
But all I needed was a magic potion.
When Christmas came,
There was no pain,
Until the Christmas play,
They all would say,
'You cannot play,
Because you are a Jew.'
The beliefs are the same,
There is no pain,
I cannot complain.
It became Christmas night,
But I could not sight
Who I wanted to see,
But then I remembered,
I'm only an evacuee.

Stacey Grix (12)
Ridgeway School

MY FOOTBALL TEAM

My football team,
I've supported them all my life.
Fast, skilled, competitive,
As good as Brazil,
Like the best team in the world,
It makes me excited when they score,
Like a four year old on a trampoline,
My football team,
Makes us remember how football is played.

Ashley Bennett (11)
Ridgeway School

JEWISH FATE

All the hundreds and thousands of Jews,
A fate worse than death, that they did not choose,
Alone, like a star in the deep, dark sky,
The disease called 'typhus' is how they would die.
German camps filled with death and grimness,
The Jews cried out with pain and distress.
A single Jew who was left on his own,
And all this because of one sick man.
Who would have known?
Like a single alien on the planet Mars,
He looked up and shouted and cried to the stars.
All the Jews had felt hunger and pain,
But to Hitler and friends, it was just a game.

Adam Brooks (13)
Ridgeway School

MY MUM

My mum is my special person
She helps me with my problems
She cooks me tea
And she takes me to see the sea
She helps me when I'm being bullied
She goes straight in, she takes no nonsense
She helps me with my homework
When she's at work I miss her
I love my mummy.

Gemma Fabiano (12)
Ridgeway School

MY SPELL POEM

My poem is to make the world out of chocolate:

Chuck in the cauldron 400 grammes of chocolate
Boil it until it is thick and creamy
Then granulate five Snickers
Pick up ten packets of Chocolate Buttons
Stir in Galaxy Caramel
Until it has dissolved
Get some cocoa powder
And chuck it in your cauldron
Get some strawberries
Leave them until they're frozen
And then chop them up
Add some Chewits Extreme
Until it is very sour
And then bake it for a long time.

Emma Pearce (12)
Ridgeway School

SPAGHETTI

S   paghetti is my favourite food
P   our it on the dish I say
A   nd make it nice and warm
G   et it down my tummy I say
H   ungry as I ever am
E   ven at school
T   wirl and wiggly I hear it say
T   ummy rumbles, the tension mounts
I   n and down it goes!

Thomas Brunskill (11)
Ridgeway School

ISOLATION

A single star in a midnight sky,
Shining bright as the hours go by,
Tomorrow will be another day,
Fighting, killing, blood all the way.

Every night I hear people cry,
For they don't have a chance to say goodbye.
Screaming, shouting, praying to God,
It's like a baby dolphin away from its pod.

I feel like something you can't explain,
With the loneliness, sadness, and the pain.
A purple man in a yellow world,
Or an orange fish alone with a girl.

I'm like a lonely alien from planet Mars,
As isolated as a single rock in the sea,
An only cat in an alley of dogs,
And a brown leaf on a forgotten tree.
Isolation.

Jessica Loveridge (12)
Ridgeway School

MY TOOTHACHE

It's really annoying
It's driving me cr zy
I want it to come out
Know it is really annoying
I want to take it out.

Charlotte Mifsud (110
Ridgeway School

ISOLATION

Alone;
As lost as a desert beneath the sun.
No one will hear your cry
As you stay still crouched against your door.
Heartbeat;
Thudding harder each time you breathe,
As the sound gets more distant,
Crying like a puppy with no home.
Fear;
Being alone whilst the war is destroying
Everything you love.
Isolation;
You whisper for your mother,
No one answers as you stand looking.
You see nothing but rubble.
As you listen, no sound enters your ears.
You're alone.
Silence;
No noise at all, your love is gone.

Rebecca Morgan (12)
Ridgeway School

MY MUM

My mum is my special person
She helps me with my homework
She sorts out all my problems
And I do all my housework
She cooks my tea, she washes my clothes
I love my mum so much
And I'll never forget her.

Kayley Mann (11)
Ridgeway School

SPELL TO BE FAMOUS

A spell for magic, a spell for charm
A spell to make you a pop star
Here are the ingredients for my spell
I'll only say if you promise not to tell
First I need some long, blonde hair
And then I'll mix in some long, fake nails
I'll add some jewellery, a diamond ring
A diamond necklace, and some crystal earrings
Kylie's attitude, Whitney Houston's voice
Victoria's dress sense and J.Lo's figure
Pour some hair dye and some make-up
Stir it together and then don't forget to shake it up.

Shaney Large (12)
Ridgeway School

MY AUNTY

My aunty died of cancer when she was 40.
She was funny, nice and quiet,
She was warm like the sun and bright like the stars,
She was also quiet like the moon creeping into the sky
                    with no one really noticing.
When I was with her she made me feel like the stars,
                    bright and happy like her,
She made me feel good and warm when I was around her.
She was my aunty.

Claire Mullard (11)
Ridgeway School

BELIEFS

Those words that deserted me for all those years,
Run like tap water through my veins.
But you're not around to hear them,
Because now you are gone.

Seven suns previous, I respected you,
For the way you lived your life.
Six moons later,
I despised you for the way you ended it.

I wish I had known your thoughts that day,
As you drove away from your home,
Away from your problems,
Away from your life.

As you crammed the mournful dust down your throat,
And took your terminal gasp of air,
You let the flames lick your branded wrists,
And the blaze take away your life, which you were so willing to give.

The salty rain that runs like rivers down my cheeks,
Leaves a muddy mark that goes from top to bottom,
Rolling off my chin, leaving a black puddle on your grave,
Reflecting the dark cloud that filled the sky and me.

Although that cloud may one day drift apart,
The reason why you did this will never become clear.
But I believed in the way you lived your life,
And although your life did, that belief will never die.

Natalie Havard (14)
Ridgeway School

ISOLATION

I woke up at this camp,
I felt like a lonely tramp,
I was trapped and couldn't get out,
I would shout and shout and shout.

I felt like dogs were chasing me,
All I wanted was to be free,
I went to an overcrowded hall,
They were being so cruel to me.

I could hear people shouting,
But then silence, I was next,
I was sweating all over,
I felt like I was dead already.

Naomi Tucker (12)
Ridgeway School

JEWISH TORTURE

Death and poor health
Poorness, no wealth
Jews crying, Jews dying
Babies burnt to a crisp
You could run away, take a risk
Or you could stay as a slave
Dig your own grave
You're going to die
There's no time to delay
So here's your choice
Run or stay.

Daniel Grayson (12)
Ridgeway School

JEWS

Like a lonely fish in the deep blue sea
I try to lose my worries in sleep
We have no choice, we cannot choose
But we are the race of Jews
Isolation is the word I use
I want to be free the same as you

Can I please, can I choose?
I really wish to be like you.
A sole planet in space
I am in the human race.
All the people look at my face
Is this really a running race?

A purple man in a yellow world
I try day by day to keep a hold
I'm an only pea in a pod
I think they think I'm a little sod
Oh they try to break my heart
But I will not be taken apart.

Ben Johnstone (12)
Ridgeway School

LONELY

I was like an island in the middle of a forgotten ocean,
As lonely as a single flower in a field,
At night I'm scared, not knowing who's there or what's happening.

Every day it's as isolated as a deserted star in the sky,
I wish I was someone else.
We are used as slaves for the fun of it,
It hurts me like a dagger in my back
Seeing other people being shot right before my eyes.

I can't describe what it's like being treated differently,
But I know inside what it's like.
We're slaving away and being shouted at and being killed,
I wish I was free.

Lauren Palmer (12)
Ridgeway School

THE CAMP

I feel as low and lonely as a mouse in a world of rats,
No one hears me, no one sees me,
I am invisible.

The cruel prickle of death creeps slowly down my spine,
The cries of protective mothers fills my ears,
In agony.

The angels of darkness come to take poor souls away,
I am a black ant in a colony of red ants,
I am outnumbered.

That day months ago when the sun ran away,
And decided never to come back again,
Total darkness.

Night is always, it is always night and never day,
Christmas came, Christmas went,
No fun.

Birthdays come, birthdays go, no celebrations,
There is no sign of movement in the camp,
Total stillness.

People have given up fighting for their freedom,
And I think very soon,
So will I.

Mikhaila Found (12)
Ridgeway School

OLD AGE

Old people drive small cars
At the speed of a tortoise
They still crash into everything
Saying 'Oh, I've hurt my back again'
Why do they have poodle dogs that look like rats
and smell like perfume?
Also, why do they complain about what they have for tea,
Saying, 'I don't like chips and mushy peas.'
They wear those smelly Marks & Spencer's woolly jumpers
With trousers which are all multicoloured.
So now you know what happens in old age.
So go to a party and start to rave,
Enjoy the years of being a kid.
So go on rides that make you dizzy and sick,
Before it's too late and you moan and your joints start to click.

O   ver 60
L   onely
D   elicate

A   ngry
G   rey
E   xcited (over dinner etc).

Martin Etheridge (14)
Ridgeway School

ONE FOR SORROW

I feel like a lonely leaf on a forgotten tree
Alone because I am different
Like a forgotten toy in a dusty attic.

I stare out of the window, all alone in the dark, cold night
One star shines brighter than the others
I wish I was somewhere else.

The scorn and laughter cuts me like a knife
Why do I have to be different?
The happiness of home seems so far away.

A flock of birds fly past
One magpie sits on its own
One for sorrow.

Ruth Bennetts (12)
Ridgeway School

A SKATEBOARD POTION

Melt the bike of Dave Mirra,
And roast the wheels to make the board fast,
Roast the legs of a cheetah for speed,
Add the power of Morris Green.

> Speed and agility, boil and bake,
> To make a famous skateboarder,
> In order, to skate.

Chad Musca's board,
The skill of Tony Hawk and Edgar Davids,
Add the fame of Slipknot and the money of Bill Gates.

> Speed and agility, boil and bake,
> To make a famous skateboarder,
> In order, to skate.

The wings of an eagle, the move of the Burntwist,
The attitude of a winner who always wants to win,
Add the stamina of Muhammad Ali.

> Speed and agility, boil and bake,
> To make a famous skateboarder,
> In order, to skate.

Jordan Page (13)
Ridgeway School

WHEN I GROW OLD

When I am old
I shall do everything
I have ever dreamed.
My children will be busy
with their young
And I will be left all on my own.
Why should I not go out and have fun?
Why should I stay in bed?
I might as well go out and enjoy myself
Since my husband Alfred's dead.

I shall swim in the sea
with dolphins,
And visit the country called Greece.
I shall parachute out
of an aeroplane,
And swim over the coral reef.
I shall go to museums and art galleries
and stay there for hours on end,
Then go home and order a pizza
and maybe share it with a friend.

Then when I fulfil all of my dreams,
I will go home and sit in bed,
Eat and drink tea and biscuits
and watch the whole series of 'Friends'.
Then I will sleep for the rest of the day
and dream of being young,
And then when I wake in the morning,
I'll do it all over again.

Laura Walker (13)
Ridgeway School

ISOLATION

As isolated as a pea in a pod
As lonely as an only cod
Isolation
As isolated as the sun in the sky
An only butterfly fluttering by
Isolation
A tree in a meadow of flowers
Being left on your own for hours
Isolation
An orange fish in a blue shoal
Trying on your own to reach your goal
Isolation
A single planet in space
A nose in the middle of a face
Isolation
As lonely as a girl isolated by boys
An only child who has no toys
Isolation
An only book in a video shop
A baby bunny trying to hop
Isolation
Everybody criticising your effort
A polar bear in the desert
Isolation
A black man surrounded by white men
Racism.

Sasha March (12)
Ridgeway School

CRUELTY TO HORSES POEM

Throw in a vet's intelligent brain,
Drizzle the mountain water in.

Stir the fresh grass of a thousand meadows,
And add a caring home.

Drop in a hoof pick for digging out the cruelty,
And sprinkle the love of a good man.

Bubble a dandy brush to get rid of the tears,
Simmer a lot of medical tools.

Soften a bag of horse food,
And roast a goal to carry on.

Then all we need is a spray of a caring home,
And to make a spell firm and good we will need a
Ban on cruelty.

Bubble, bubble, kindness and loving,
Stir and stir and then it's working.

Lucy Westgarth (12)
Ridgeway School

CHRISTMAS TIME

It was Christmas time again,
And the lights were as bright as could be,
As we entered the hall,
We saw the stage,
And upon it stood Miss Thorne.

She called me over and sat me down,
And told me to go on home.
I wondered why,
And she said it was because I'm a Jew.

Every day I went to watch,
And I grew more and more used to it,
But the thing that was wrong was,
My best friend had taken my place.

I never saw my friends,
Especially young Willie; I was always alone,
Sitting in the house thinking to myself,
When will I see him again?

Paul Sowden (12)
Ridgeway School

ZACH THE JEW

The teacher said 'I'm joking,'
Trying to be in the Christmas play.

The teacher thought I was choking,
When I started acting my lines.

My best friend got the part instead,
I almost went and lost my head.

I found out it's because I'm a Jew!

The world's as biased as a two-headed coin,
Just because of the race you're born into.

Little Weirwold where I'm staying,
Writing, reading, even playing.

While some Jews suffer in pain,
I sleep in bed safe and sane.

The worst of things are in Germany,
While I'm sat here writing poetry.

Darren Edge (12)
Ridgeway School

A Spell For The Perfect Footballer

First we shall grate the training of Sir Alex Ferguson,
Then sprinkle the leadership of Alan Shearer.
Grate some of Bobby Charlton's experience,
Fourth we shall whisk his brother Jack's tackles.

Bubble and bake, spin and stir,
Turn this into a great footballer.

We shall throw in some of Bosnich's saves,
And sizzle David Beckham's free-kicks.
Add some of Michael Owen's speed,
And some of David Seaman's long kicks.

Bubble and bake, spin and stir,
Turn this into a great footballer.

Add some of Andy Cole's popularity,
Then some of Edgar David's skill.
Finish off with a pinch of Man U's gold.

Aaron Perrin (12)
Ridgeway School

Isolation

Isolation is loneliness,
When walls close in around you,
You're different from everyone else,
And everyone is different from you.

Isolation is single,
Like the last leaf on a tree,
Like an only bird in the sky,
No one looks at me.

Isolation is hidden,
Beneath the roaring waves,
Under the earth's surface,
Lost in dark, damp caves.

Isolation is lost,
Like the last pea in a pod,
Like an only flower in a meadow,
I feel like I am odd.

Sarah Pengilly (12)
Ridgeway School

MY SPELL POEM

Go away, disappear, I don't want anyone
here.
In the cauldron goes Mum's necklace, Dad's tie
and laughter of children.
Go away, disappear, I don't want anyone
here.
Boil and burn the money of millions,
Throw in some clothes from the
wardrobe.
Go away, disappear, I don't want anyone
here.
Add the cold of a winter and the heat of a
summer,
Get a leaf from the ground in the
autumn.
Go away, disappear, I don't want anyone
here.
Now I'm free, free to myself.

Emma Rowe (12)
Ridgeway School

ISOLATION

I woke up and smelt the horrible smell of dead bodies rotting,
The smell of gas from the concentration camp.
I woke up to hear the screaming of children who had lost their parents,
I would shout and shout and try to get out.

I was cold and helpless, hungry and scared,
The soldiers kept shouting and shouting at me,
But I just turned away to flee.
The food they gave us was nothing but bread,
The people around us looked up in disgust at the way they were
                                                           being treated.

They took my mum away, I pulled them away,
But they hit me back.
I screamed for her and shouted for her,
But they took her right in the concentration camp.
The screaming and shouting I heard deep inside,
It stopped and I knew that she was dead.

I started to cry and cry and cry,
My dad came over and comforted me but it didn't make me feel
                                                           any better.
The soldiers came over and took my dad away,
I kept saying, 'No, no, no.'
They pushed me away, the shouting and screaming, again it came.
The end of my life started today.

Natalie Peters (13)
Ridgeway School

MY CAULDRON POEM

Cook the hand of Peter Schmeichel,
Sprinkle the speed of Maurice Green,
Beat the tackle of Tony Adams,
Burn the power of Roy Keane,
Crush the curl of David Beckham,
Blend in the skill of Michael Owen,
Melt the wiseness of Alex Ferguson,
Roast the awareness of Paul Scholes,
Pour the heading power of Alan Shearer,
Freeze the reaction of Jaap Stam,
Stir the acrobatics of Fabian Barthez,
Boil the glove of David Seaman.

David Foster (13)
Ridgeway School

FRIENDS

Friends are people who really care
They touch your heart and will always be there
They make you feel good whenever you're down
And reassure you when you're not around.

Someone out there will realise
The only people on our minds
Are the people we defend
Those people being our friends
My heart breaks when I fall out
So where would we be without our friends
They will be there until the end.

April Stephens (12)
Ridgeway School

MY SPELL TO MAKE ME THE BEST AT EVERYTHING

Make the cauldron fire,
Above all the rest,
It'll make me the very best,
It's bubbling very tall,
Higher than my bedroom wall

Leg of a cheetah,
To make me very fast,
That way I'll never come last.
Head of an owl,
So I could look around,
I could see every sight,
And hear every sound.

Make the cauldron fire,
Above all the rest,
It'll make me the very best,
It's bubbling very tall,
Higher than my bedroom wall

The eyes of a cat,
The wings of a bat,
The jaws of a snake,
And the power of an earthquake,
All added together,
Including the force of the weather,
Will make me the *best!*

Make the cauldron fire,
Above all the rest,
It'll make me the very best,
It's bubbling very tall,
Higher than my bedroom wall

Lloyd Brewer (12)
Ridgeway School

A SUPER HERO SPELL

Beat the hearing till it's sharp
And fold into the knowledge
Sprinkle in a pinch of boldness
And add a spoonful of courage

Bubble, boil and bake
Simmer, sizzle and shake
Easy-peasy, piece of cake
A super hero to make

Drain the braveness of Batman
And spoon out the speed of Spiderman
Mix with the strength of Superman
And stir in the ability of Action Man

Bubble, boil and bake
Simmer, sizzle and shake
Easy-peasy, piece of cake
A super hero to make

Heat the wisdom of an owl
And add the toughness of a rhino
Pour in the eyesight of an eagle
And now we have our super hero

Bubble, boil and bake
Simmer, sizzle and shake
Easy-peasy, piece of cake
A super hero to make

Christian Woods (12)
Ridgeway School

THE F1 SPELL (FOR DRIVER AND CAR)

For the perfect driver's gift,
you will have to search and sift,
for the perfect gift now,
use the ingredients in order shown,
confidence of Michael Shumacher,
reactions of Ayrton Senna,
now you're feeling a lot better,
carry on to get even *better,*
tacticional uses of Ross Brawn,
good sportsmanship of Mika Hakkinen,
all these ingredients in the oven bake,
till small enough and ready to take,
then sprinkle on top the emotions of a songbird,
now you are ready to join the herd.

But now time to make the car,
and you are now really far,
take a pinch of Marinello,
and the sheer roar of the Ferrari's bellow,
then steal the aerodynamics of an eagle,
upon now it begins to sizzle,
sprinkle on top the Ferrari's speed,
this car will take you far into the lead,
and now the car is nearly ready,
this car will run smooth and steady,
the last ingredient is the spirit of the crowd,
it is now sure that you will take the crown!

Joshua Trust (12)
Ridgeway School

MY NEW SNOOKER SKILLS

Bake Fergal O'Brien's cue
Add a dash of John Higgins' cue action
Roast Jimmy White's popularity
Add a twist of Andy Hicks' public outings
Drizzle Mark Williams' money
Pour Ronnie O'Sullivan's trophies
Boil Mark King's waistcoats
Deep-fry Matthew Stevens' coach
Grill John Parrot's England captaincy
Cook Quinton Hann's accent
Mix in Joe Swail's disabilities
Fry Peter Ebdon's colour blindness
Whisk in Ronnie O'Sullivan's personal problems
Bubble Stephen Hendry's skills
Last of all bake Steve Davis' experience.

Matthew J Draper (12)
Ridgeway School

SPELL OF STONE CURSE

Half a stone, quarter of rock,
Make the spell snip and snap.
Diamond of a dragon,
Bladder stones make the spell
As hard as bones.
Drizzle and drop some sizzling sapphires,
Red ruby eyes that are as hot as fire.
Sizzle, snap, stir and mix,
So the spell goes to bricks.

Luke West (12)
Ridgeway School

A Spell To Make Everyone In The World As Kind As Father Christmas

Pour the snow from the North Pole,
Smell the reindeer,
Cook the presents,
Fry the carrots,
Sprinkle the stars,
Chop the white bears,
Melt the songs of praise,
Boil the bright night,
Freeze the sleigh until it cracks,
Bake the suit and boil the belt,
Toast the thoughts
And mash the kindness,
Stir it round and blend in the sauce.

Sarah Humphries (12)
Ridgeway School

A Spell Poem To Be A Fish

Beat a shark's fin,
Fry the barracuda's body until crispy,
Grate the tentacles of a jellyfish,
Cook a mantle ray's mouth,
Sprinkle the electric shock of an eel,
Burn the teeth of a piranha,
Pour the sea salt water into the cauldron until sizzling hot,
Add the seaweed to the shark's speediness,
Then toast the hawk's eyes until hard,
Last of all add the nose of a lion,
Then simmer until it smells good.

Martyn Welsh (13)
Ridgeway School

A SPELL TO BECOME THE BEST FOOTBALL PLAYER IN THE WORLD

Roast the shirt of the Liverpool team,
Pour in the save of Barthez,
Throw in the header of Teddy Sheringham,
Add the skill of Edgar Davids,
Knead the talent of George Best,
And grate the experience of Sir Geoff Hurst,
Whisk the money of the England team,
Separate the boots of Louis Figo,
Place in the captain's band of bald-headed Beckham,
And throw in the speed of Roberto Carlos,
Beat the dribbling of Ryan Giggs,
Drizzle the tackle and strength of Stam,
and simmer that strike of Kluivert,
And the sportsmanship of little Zola,
And deep-fry the big mouth of Robbie Keane,
Spin the back heel of Harry Kewell,
And blend the keep-ups of Ronaldo,
Melt the curl of the amazing Batistuta,
Crack in the chest of Zidane,
Grate the football used in the final of the UEFA Cup,
And freeze the spectacular finish of Michael Owen,
Burn the classical control of Kanu,
And defrost the brain and determination of Gerrard,
Spray the stamina of Sammi Hyppia,
And peel the fantastic Sven Goran Eriksson,
Dash the top class teamwork of Liverpool,
Flip the chasing back of Veron,
Bake the gigantic long throw from Gary Neville,
Soften the overhead kick of Ronaldo,
Cut up the hundreds of headers of Costa.

Jack Gamble (12)
Ridgeway School

A PERFECT FOOTBALLER

Roast the shirt of Ruud Van Nistelrooy,
Pour in the speed of Ryan Giggs,
Beat the header of Teddy Sheringham,
Add the save of Fabian Barthez,
Knead the experience of George Best,
Whisk the money of Roy Keane,
Put in the determination of Steven Gerrard,
Throw in the passing of Veron,
Drop in the captaincy of Sol Campbell,
Add the sportsmanship of Gary Neville,
Drop in the control of Kanu,
Peel the brain of Paul Scholes,
Add the keep-ups of Luis Figo,
Whisk the chasing back of Veron,
Add the strike of Dennis Bergkamp,
Pour in the finish of wonder boy Owen,
Throw in the free-kick of David Beckham,
Pour in the curl of Roberto Carlos,
Add the tackling of Colin Hendry,
Sprinkle on the strength of Emile Heskey.
Now you have a perfect footballer.

Mark Cooney (13)
Ridgeway School

ATHLETE SPELL

Roast legs of cheetah
Toast eagles' wings,
Blend paper money
Sizzle legs of Jonathan Edwards.

Long jump, short jump
100m sprint, 50m hurdle
and then leave a print.

Mix power of Maurice Green
Simmer Denise Lewis's gold medal,
Grate intelligence of Paula Ratcliffe
Burn fuel of Concorde.

Long jump, short jump
100m spring, 50m hurdle
and then leave a print.

Nick Bunczuk (12)
Ridgeway School

A SPELL FOR A LIFETIME'S SUPPLY OF CHOCOLATE

Grate 400g of chocolate,
Microwave a competition winner,
Burn a shop then boil,
Drizzle a bit of salad dressing,
Then blend in a pack of greasy nuts,
Mix in raisins, then stir,
Freeze a chocolate machine,
Grill an entry form,
Blend in 2 pints of milk,
Pour in some cocoa powder,
Add in a few drops of caramel,
Simmer in 10 pounds of sugar,
Mash in some biscuits,
Melt 200g of butter,
Throw in some flour,
Whisk in a whole lot of luck,
Chop in some coconut,
Add in a pinch of salt,
Then mix this all together and you should have a perfect
recipe for a spell to have a life's supply of chocolate.

Samantha Marlow (13)
Ridgeway School

A Dream Once Existed, You Were Mine, Are Mine

A dream once existed.
Wind twined through roses,
Sun hung onto the mirrored vision of the ocean.
Eyes trapped in a willing gaze;
so intense,
so passionate,
so lust-worthy,

all mine.

Tonight to exist in only a misted dream,
From tomorrow and onward,
As I crumble from unwanted nightmare turned real.
Your kiss,
your touch,
your warmth and passion,

everlastingly mine.

It seems not lasting, you vanish from our world,

now.

Alone, not laughing, singing, making no dance of love.
Tears drip, trickle down trembled lips.
My lips touched yours, your hands touched mine;
they were warm,
were capturing,
were love,

were to touch me when blue, marked mine.

A dream once existed,
a world called yours and mine.
The roses still sway and dance, the sun still glistens, the gaze
now set all around,
But all the while, the beauty is not noticed without your presence
to complete.
I'm going crazy, missing you baby,
living without you.
Truly and deeply I love you,
Until I gaze upon your scent again, stronger than ever,

my love will be yours.

Yours will be mine.

Forever. Completely mine!

Kate Moss (14)
Ridgeway School

A SPELL TO HELP ME SPELL

Chop up a dictionary,
Then sprinkle in the ABC
Then microwave alphabet spaghetti
While getting the bread ready
Then slip in the Brain of Britain
While whisking in a genius's knowledge
Add a teacher's answer book
While the cauldron bubbles and spits
Get a spoon and mix it quick.

Kayleigh Mackey (12)
Ridgeway School

ETERNITY STARS OF LUCK TO WILD PONIES

Twist in a soul of a happy child
Grate in a dandelion leaf with
Glimmering dew.
Add a slurp of salty sea rain
Then our spell is working good

Boil, boil, toast and fry
Make the evil say goodbye.

Gently throw in a golden eagle's feather
Smoothly blow in the confidence of a lion
Quickly flick in a cat's slashing claw
Then we're getting somewhere now

Boil, boil, toast and fry
Make the evil say goodbye

Sprinkle in a little girl's night tears
Add sap of an old tree
Gently toss in a frog with no fear
Know it's sizzling firm and good

Boil, boil, toast and fry
Make the evil say goodbye

Last but not least, add a glimpse of the North Star
And add the light of the sun
Now the horses have got happiness
Because my spell has brought health

Boil, boil, toast and fry
Make the evil say goodbye.

Emily Chapman (12)
Ridgeway School

WHEN I REALISED YOU WEREN'T THERE

Do you know how strange it was, when I realised you weren't there?
No more jokes that weren't funny, but made me laugh.
No more war stories that fascinated me.
No more 'When I was a boy' punch lines.

Do you know how strange it was, when I realised you weren't there?
When I stared at the chair you used to sit on,
And the place at the dinner table where you used to eat.
When I looked at the picture of you on your wedding day.
I smiled.

Do you know how strange it was, when I realised you weren't there?
When I look at the photos of when I was a baby, and saw you in them.
Remember?
You would give me piggybacks and wheel me around in your
wheelbarrow.
You would play tennis and football with me.
You would tell me bedtime stories, about talking farm animals.
I laughed.

Do you know how strange it was, when I realised you weren't there?
When I realised I couldn't say goodbye to you,
When I realised I could never talk to you again,
When I realised I could never see you again,
And all I could do was cry.

When I realised you weren't there.

Nikki Houston (15)
Ridgeway School

BROKEN

Dearly beloved we are gathered here today,
To join these two people in holy matrimony,
'I do'
'I don't'

Broken.
How can a love so strong be crushed?
Like a china plate plummeting towards the ground,
With the clicking of a finger.

The harsh words spoken,
Never taken back.
The love vanishes,
Into the landscape.

No feeling,
Numb,
Shivering with fear,
Speechless.

You're out of sight,
You seem out of mind,
Careless,
Love is for never.

The future seems vivid,
Yet Sundays come soon,
The hurt grows,
The hurt stays.

Think.
But I don't want to,
Yet it stays in your mind,
Like death.

Emma Hagan (14)
Ridgeway School

BUNDLE OF JOY

As I look down at my bundle of joy
It makes my body melt.
Those big blue eyes look back at me
And I have a feeling inside that I have never felt.

Let me get close to you,
To hold you tight.
I could read you stories
And tuck you in at night.

Let me be your friend,
To help you with your troubles.
I could be your shoulder to cry on
And give you loads of cuddles.

Let me be your light,
When you wake up with a scream.
I could sit beside you
And help you through your dream.

Let me be there for you,
Throughout all your years.
I could be the one
That wipes away all your tears.

Let me care for you,
And look after your health,
Until you're strong enough
To look after yourself.

Rachael Gregory (14)
Ridgeway School

SPELL FOR WORLD PEACE

Pluck a feather from a calm, golden duck
Watch the feather float into the pot
Burn all the guns in the world
Fry all the daggers to a crisp
Take a bullet from a graceful man's heart
Steam the blood of a pure saint
Throw in the splintery cross of Jesus
Mix in a crown of bloody thorns
From a man's head
Soften a kind woman's heart
Drop in a branch of a colourful, burning tree
Stew leaves from the naked Adam and Eve
Chop up a mouth from a swearing man
Whisk the wool of a cuddly lamb
Knead a piece of cloud from the happy, daytime sky
Flip the brightest star in the beautiful night sky
Toast a piece of the holy Pope's cloth
Dice the toe of helpful Mother Teresa
Then peace will enter the world.

Justine Bainbridge (12)
Ridgeway School

MONEY

Money, money, money, ain't I funny,
I help you pay your bills,
You put me in the bank then I take control,
You save me, you spend me, you even invest me,
I even drive people round the bend.

I'm green and cool and sometimes hot,
So hot I'll burn a hole in your money pot.

Christopher Symons & Thomas Body (11)
Ridgeway School

TAKEN AWAY

You were here, and then you were suddenly put there
It came and took you away, away from us all
It didn't ask consent, it just snatched you away.

Then you were gone, gone too soon.

It came like a lightning bolt from out the sky
Struck you down and removed you from this world
Removed you from my life.

The blossom on the trees reminds me of you,
Bringing joy to me and been swept too far away,
To make my life empty and dark.

I still can't believe you've gone, you've gone too soon.

You were like a warm sunbeam, your smiley face, those loving eyes,
The way you looked after me when I was ill, now it's all gone to dust
Never to be seen again on this earth.

You didn't deserve it, it was pure evil, and I wish every day
That I'd had the chance to say goodbye,
But it came too quick and took you away from me.

Rebecca Tomlinson (14)
Ridgeway School

MY NEW CLASSROOM

Would have a swimming pool next door
And a nice soft carpet on the floor
So we won't need our shoes anymore.

Thomas Snell (12)
Woodlands School

DARRYL'S DREAM CLASSROOM

My room would be a big sports hall,
We'd play snooker and football.
I'd like a full-size football pitch
And visits from Man U, Ipswich,
Arsenal, West Ham.
Liverpool would visit too,
That's really cool.

I'd also like a big sand pit,
And a mega, real drum kit.
I could make a load of noise.
I also want some football toys,
Egg and chips for lunch for me,
Then I'd go home for my tea.

Darryl Saunders (12)
Woodlands School

FANTASY CLASSROOM

A glass door
a pink floor

Plastic sinks
lots of drinks

A pink chair
nice fresh air

No rubbish
a dog and some fish

My list ends
with me and my friends.

Victoria Cusack (12)
Woodlands School